Second Edition

# Kaanish Belvaspata

---

## Healing Modality of Enlightenment

---

**For Enlightenment Levels 1 through 5**

## Almine

Published by Spiritual Journeys LLC

Second Edition October, 2009
First Edition May, 2009


Copyright 2009
MAB 998 Megatrust


By Almine
Spiritual Journeys LLC
P.O. Box 300
Newport, Oregon 97365

www.spiritualjourneys.com

Cover Illustration — Dorian Dyer
Book Production — Ariel Frailich
Editor — Jan Alvey


Manufactured in the United States of America


ISBN 978-1-934070-44-4

# Table of Contents

# Acknowledgements

This book is dedicated to Jan. For her beautiful and luminous presence in my life and her tireless support, I am eternally grateful.

Thank you to Eva for the beautiful artwork of the wheels.

Cover Art: Dorian Dyer
www.visionheartart.com

# About the Author

Almine is endorsed and described as one of the greatest mystics of our time by world leaders and scientists alike. While other way-showers gather more and more students, she helps create more and more masters. Her work represents the cutting edge of mysticism; that place where the physical and the non-physical meet and new realities are born. It is here where change is rapid and insight comes quickly to wash away years of stagnation.

In February of 2005, Almine's body underwent a transfiguration, changing from mortal to immortal in the twinkling of an eye. Her books have been a roadmap to lead others into the same mastery and beyond. Masters populate her classes and are a fulfillment of a mission given to her in January 2005: prepare the leadership for a Golden Age about to be birthed on Earth.

Having lived as a Toltec Nagual (a specific type of mystic dedicated to a life of impeccability and setting others free from illusion) for most of her life, her insights into cosmology and man's role within the macrocosm are ground-breaking. Pushing illuminating insights even further than previous Toltecs have done, she has managed to solve mysteries that have perplexed seers for eons.

Throughout history, the majority of spiritual masters and gurus who have entered mastery have withdrawn from society. This is understandable because words seem inadequate to describe experiences such as coming face-to-face with the Infinite and the physical act of speaking becomes laborious. Almine's gift is her ability to convey these experiences by rendering the unspeakable understandable. She feels it is time for people to understand that they can choose to claim mastery as their constant reality and remain functional in society.

Words to describe the unknowable flow through her and when shared with others often leave them feeling as though they have touched the face of God. Her revelations bring answers to questions that have plagued mankind since the dawn of time, revealing the origin and meaning of human existence.

Her journey has become one of learning to live in the physical while functioning in eternal time and maintaining the delicate balance of remaining self-aware while being fully expanded.

# Introduction

During the final quarter of 2008, I was instructed by the Infinite to prepare 14 different websites – each containing the equivalent of at least half a book of information, freely available to all. Deep mystical techniques were given from many ancient and sacred traditions – many of which had over the eons either lost their potency and power or their purity.

The purpose for this renaissance of incorruptible and powerful information had not been clear to me until the first week of February 2009. For the first time, Belvaspata and other previously separate bodies of information started weaving together. The restoration of the mastery and incorruptible magic to man that is his birthright seemed to be the overall purpose.

During the last week of January 2009, a huge compound of pyramids and towers, connected by circular tunnels, was discovered by myself and the oracle Eva, after we were led to it by the angels. The structure had been built by the angels with the assistance of Isis and a group known as the Zhong-galabruk (the Cat people).

Among the many priceless secrets, devices and revelations were the components needed to construct a set of up to 24 gates through which beneficial influences could be sent on a large scale.

With the simple construction of these gates in their homes, Belvaspata masters could now make a very profound impact on the well-being of the Earth and its creatures. But shortly after receiving Kaanish Belvaspata, the Belvaspata of Enlightenment, another marriage of information took place: Belvaspata sigils to use with the complete Toltec body healing system. Yet again there was an integration of two entirely separate healing modalities for greatly enhanced results.

It is clear that the age of empowerment of those who have wished to render service in purity and with power, has dawned. The tools are in our hands. Angels have been called to assist us. With dedication in our hearts, let us embrace the spiritual maturity we have earned and truly become the light beacons of the Earth.

To the Infinite One Life the Glory Forever,
Almine

# Kaanish Belvaspata

## The Healing Modality of Enlightenment
(literal translation: the cosmic proxy Belvaspata)

With the advent of this Belvaspata, a few notable changes have occurred: The master and grandmaster initiations may be performed simultaneously. Second, this unique form of Belvaspata, representing the high mind, has come forth to be used by qualified masters of Belvaspata at all levels.

- The level I and level II Belvaspata masters represent the healing of the sub-conscious or low mind.
- The masters and grandmasters represent the healing of the middle-mind (the left and right brain).
- The Kaanish Belvaspata is the healing modality representing the high mind.

### HOW DOES IT WORK?

Every sigil of Kaanish Belvaspata represents the cosmos. When used by a Belvaspata master of any level, the recipient is a proxy for the cosmic well-being. Such great service must be compensated for by dramatic increases in consciousness.

When it is used, which can be done as part of a usual Belvaspata session or as a separate session to benefit cosmic life, the recipient will also reap physical benefits. There does not need to be an ailment for Kaanish Belvaspata to be done.

The gift of physical healing regular Belvaspata brings is now supplemented by the advent of Kaanish Belvaspata as an enhancer of consciousness.

## IS IT FREE?

Almine, the originator of regular Belvaspata, has given it freely as a gift. Kaanish Belvaspata and other advanced (specialty) Belvaspata are available through the purchase of a manual and other products from the website www.belvaspata.org. Although anyone can purchase the manual, it is intended for the use of Belvaspata masters only.

## ARE INITIATIONS REQUIRED TO PERFORM IT?

None other than the initiations and self-initiations regular Belvaspata masters undergo. As always it is requested that you credit Almine as the originator of this profound work designed to set man free from illusion.

**All levels of Belvaspata masters may use the sigils in this Belvaspata manual without any further initiation.** The Belvaspata Initiation and Healing Manual in *Belvaspata Initiation Starter Kit 1* is a recommended reference and guide for the use of Belvaspata, available for purchase on www.belvaspata.org.

# HOW TO USE ADVANCED BELVASPATA

**Any advanced (specialty) Belvaspata may be used in conjunction with a basic Belvaspata session.** Begin advanced Belvaspata following the initial session. Follow any specific directions provided for each type of Belvaspata.

### USE OF ADVANCED BELVASPATA FOR SELF, OR WITH ANOTHER INDIVIDUAL

1.  Open the session with an expansion process, holding expanded awareness as you feel is appropriate, suggested 5-10 minutes.

2. Proceed with any other advanced Belvaspata; see additional titles available on www.belvaspata.org.
3. Always end a session by signing the sigils for love, praise and gratitude; this materializes the healing intentions and pulls awareness in.

*The information in this book is not intended to diagnose illness or to constitute medical advice or treatment. All healing takes place within self.*

*Please follow all regulatory guidelines of your specific municipality in terms of assisting others, even with their express consent. A physician should be consulted for any necessary medical attention.*

# The Illusions that Fractured the DNA of Man

## THE FORMATION OF THE ROSE

The following information is an excerpt from the first month of Almine's online course *Academy of Alchemy – Tools of Illumination*.

The rose pattern, indicating the sound or frequency chambers of the DNA of man, is the kaleidoscope lens mentioned as part of the seven illusions, later in the book. The cosmic sound chambers are the reflection of the Infinite's DNA and follow a similar pattern.

In the last few days of January 2009, the answers to healing the separation consciousness of man found in his DNA presented itself. A body of information called Kaanish Belvaspata was received: a healing modality to bring enlightenment.

But the way in which it brings enlightenment was not initially clear as the first 14 hours of information was transcribed. It was only during the last 10 hours, which came a few days later, that a pattern started to reveal itself: we were healing the illusions that fractured the DNA of man, restoring its pristine nature.

This is why it was emphatically stressed to me that the steps to be followed when doing Kaanish Belvaspata had to be done in the order given. The DNA strand has to be healed, its fractured petals blended into one from the inside out. The effect of writing down the sigils and angels was profound. The light in the room was golden then white. My hands seemed transparent and sometimes the pen as well – a truly magnificent experience.

# HEALING THE ROWS OF PETALS IN THE DNA ROSE

## ENLIGHTENMENT LEVELS I AND II

The research of many behavioral scientists has indicated that man seems to have a 'pain body' – a layer of magnetic frequencies that carry memories of pain. This resembles the memory of someone's voice on the magnetic strip of an audiotape that can be replayed over and over again.

During 2008 a great deal had been done by the Infinite to remove the memory of separation by eliminating the electrical grids of the cosmos, as well as the matrices. But the cosmic pain body, the magnetic matrix, had not been dissolved.

The pain body originates from the DNA strand, where it lies like a surrounding sheath of magnetic frequencies containing memories of pain and trauma. The first two levels remove this.

## ENLIGHTENMENT LEVEL III

This level clears rows 3, 7, 12 and 20 of the petals of the DNA rose of their separations by dispelling the core illusions that caused them in the first place.

ROW OF 3 PETALS
For the removal of the illusions of space, duality and polarity.

ROW OF 7 PETALS
For the removal of the 7 cosmic illusions of the mirror, the rainbow, the echo, the mirage, the lens, the kaleidoscope lens and the cosmic vacuum created by clustering as a way to create.

ROW OF 12 PETALS
These sigils remove the 7 shadow casters of Inaccessible Potential, Wisdom, the fractured DNA, the traditions and nationalism form-

ing soul patterns, the illusion of external information, the building blocks of life, the illusion of accomplishment.

ROW OF 20 PETALS
The last portion of level III corrects illusions around the perfection of life's unfoldment; the illusion of the mistakes of life. The misperceptions removed are:

1. That life's stressors make some stronger but are more than others can bear, cracking them and that there are victims of too much stress
2. That we have been conditionally loved; approved only when we are 'good'
3. That we are imperfectly made and then punished if we do not succeed
4. That we should have more abilities than what we do have
5. That Creation is formed through trial and error
6. That the purpose of Creation is for the Infinite to learn and experience discovery of Its Being
7. That there are flaws in the timing of when certain things happen

## ENLIGHTENMENT LEVEL IV

THE ROW OF 33 PETALS
For the removal of the 3 primary causes of victimhood:

The illusions that
1. Unfairness and inequity exist
2. We are exploited or used as a resource by the Infinite
3. That the cosmos is haphazardly or inexpertly handled

# The Enhanced Rose Template

THE ROW OF 54 PETALS

The sigils related to this portion eliminate the seven causes of hopelessness:

1. That we are given unfair standards to live by
2. That the pace is too fast or too slow
3. That there is an unfair amount of responsibility placed on us
4. That life is a part of a tyrannical system with not enough allowance for us to self-express
5. That there are unrealistic expectations of us
6. That we're blocked from flourishing rather than supported
7. Life is to be endured rather than enjoyed

THE ROW OF 72 PETALS

This eliminates the three primary causes of fear:

1. Fear of failure through inadequacy
2. Fear of missing something we should know or do
3. Fear of not seeing and making the right choices

THE ROW OF 96 PETALS

This final section of Part IV eliminates the seven causes of agony that lie as obsolete programming in the DNA:

1. The illusion that we can be separated from what we love
2. Feelings of being misplaced; as though we don't belong here
3. Feeling there should be an end to the journey
4. Living on the edge, vulnerable, as though bad things could happen at any time
5. Feeling that home is an external place
6. Feeling that we don't have a place where our unique gifts can be expressed, appreciated or understood
7. Feeling unprotected against harm

## ENLIGHTENMENT LEVEL V

THE ROW OF 144 PETALS
This portion instills the 3 attitudes of surrender:
1. Surrendering to the moment
2. Taking full responsibility of what we manifest in our environment
3. Surrendering to our inner guidance

THE ROW OF 214 PETALS
There is only one extremely powerful sigil for the wholeness of the self through the embodiment of the 144 self-wheels.

THE ROW OF 300 PETALS
There is only one sigil for the embodiment of inner peace and contentment. The sigil creates the embodiment of the 4 Wheels of Inner Peace.

*THE FOUR WHEELS OF INNER PEACE*
1. Delighting in the flow of change
2. Living in the light of complete self-honesty
3. Living in the perfect harmonious inner integration
4. Finding a cherishing inner home

THE ROW OF 514 PETALS
There is one sigil for the embodying of the Thirteen Wheels of the Manifestation of Majesty.

*13 WHEELS OF MANIFESTATION OF MAJESTY*
1. Letting our light shine to the fullest
2. Expecting miracles with hearts of hope
3. Acknowledging our Divine Heritage as Creations of the Infinite
4. Embracing our Divine Perfection

5. Seeing our beauty and majesty reflected in nature
6. Knowing all life lives within us
7. Claiming all knowledge and effortless knowing
8. Living in the sovereignty of self-expression
9. Taking full responsibility for the quality of each moment
10. Living with the glory of Elegance
11. Pleasing our heart first, that giving may come from fullness
12. Dedicating our lives to being the embodiment of Immortal Glory
13. Living each moment majestically

**Summary**: When the partitions of the Rose's petals are removed, we live in total oneness – the god-kingdom. The One Wheel That Contains All symbolizes this and is the design found on the floor of the central round chamber of Isis in the massive and complex compound of angel magic (known as the Wheel of Life) in the sands of Egypt. The nucleus of the DNA has become one with all the petals.

# The 4 Wheels of Inner Peace

## WHEEL OF INNER PEACE 1

### Delighting in the flow of change

# WHEEL OF INNER PEACE 2

## Living in the Light of Complete Self-honesty

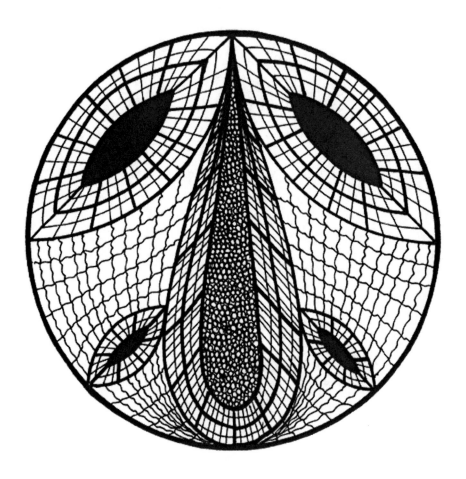

# WHEEL OF INNER PEACE 3

## Living in the Perfect Harmonious Inner Integration

# WHEEL OF INNER PEACE 4

## Finding a Cherishing Inner Home

# The 13 Wheels of the Manifestation of Mastery

Letting our Light Shine to the Fullest

1

Expecting Miracles with Hearts of Hope

2

Acknowledging our Divine Heritage as Creations of the Infinite

3

Embracing our Divine Perfection

4

## Seeing our Beauty and Majesty reflected in Nature

5

## Knowing All Lives within Us

6

## Claiming All Knowledge and Effortless Knowing

7

## Living in the Sovereignty of self-expression

8

# Taking Full Responsibility for the Quality of each Moment

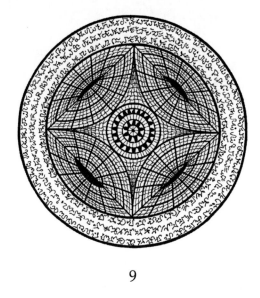

9

# Living with the Glory of Elegance

10

Pleasing our Hearts First, that Giving may come from Fullness

11

Dedicating our Lives to Being the Embodiment of Immortal Glory

12

## Living each Moment Majestically

13

# From the Library of the Angels

The DNA of all races combine in that of man
Like the ends of many strings he holds in his hands
Tablets of light, written in gold
Shall bring man powers of angels to hold

A few shall stand forth, with love in their hearts
Then great changes among men shall start
As systems destructure and tyranny fails
Hope they will bring of a better way

No more shall men labor while only a few gain
Angel sigils shall heal humankind's pain
When all wavers, succumb not to fear
Call through the angels and assistance is near.

# BOOK ONE

Kaanish Belvaspata

# Enlightenment Level I

## PAARA-HIRUVAT

The angel for fluid and graceful change through
Kaanish Belvaspata Level I

**Note:** Before starting a level of Kaanish Belvaspata, look at the sigil of the angel for fluid and graceful change for that specific level. Call the name of the angel and say:

"By the power of your sigil that I hold, I call on you to create a fluid and graceful process of purification and enlightenment through level I of Kaanish Belvaspata."

1.  **Belshi-etprevaa-harustraa**

*Angel name:*
**Kiresparvi**

For the healing of the subconscious mind

2.  **Pluhat-verbis-uvastaba**

*Angel name:*
**Nu-avesbi**

For the healing of the middle mind

3.  **Krach-bahar-ustaba**

*Angel name:*
**Nunaveshbi-strauhar**

For the healing of the higher mind

In Kaanish Belvaspata all sigils are proxy sigils, in that they are automatically done for the cosmos – thereby blessing the person giving and receiving (all) with gifts of enlightenment.

**4. Plihabak-velvesh-aruna**

*Angel name:*
**Kistebaruk**

For the balancing of masculine and feminine components in mind

**5. Bru-abak-setlvi**

*Angel name:*
**Kurasastrava**

For clear communication between electrical and magnetic
components within mind and the body

**6. Vrubranik-salvavesbi**

*Angel name:*
**Establanish-veravi**

For the unconditional oneness of all minds

**7. Kelhavi-skavel-urespavi**

*Angel name:*
**Nichtunenheshvi**

For the opening of mind to Infinite Presence

**8. Virut-helvis-estravaa**

*Angel name:*
**Klunechbashbi**

For clarity of awareness

**9. Spu-aretnushet-vavi**

*Angel name:*
**Agnasta-bluavet**

For establishing reference points during expansion

**10. Kuha-avasta-pli-aha**

*Angel name:*

**Kinesta-plava**

For removing fear for survival from the middle mind

**11. Tru-bilechspa-kabelhut**

*Angel name:*

**Ustrava**

For removing fear for survival from the sub-conscious mind

**12. Vrupalik-stuanut-vestabi**

*Angel name:*

**Nunasbi**

For removing fear for survival from internal organs

**13. Kaalsh-hik-servatu**

*Angel name:*

**Eres-tranunit**

For removing of the constrictive response from muscles

**14. Kurutbalas-vershvabi**

*Angel name:*

**Michpa-nunetvi**

For instilling humor into the muscle groups to promote surrender

**15. Paartlhut-skluvechva**

*Angel name:*

**Mishvel-splara**

For removing the tendency of joints to lock,
as an emergency response

## 16. Blu-anushpavaa-hesvi

*Angel name:*
**Kinig-stetvi**

To remove the fight or flight response from internal organs

## 17. Kluvaruk-erestava

*Angel name:*
**Biletrekvi**

To remove the fight or flight response from muscles

## 18. Kurutnunestu

*Angel name:*
**Pli-eshbrakbi**

To remove fight or flight response from joints

**19. Kaaretnunherspaa**

*Angel name:*

**Pitribilechskla**

To remove from the heart, the memory of traumatic creation

**20. Kaararat-arasnanat-vavi**

*Angel name:*

**Ustubalechvi**

To remove fear of the unknown from the mind

**21. Aaras-bravabish-huvra**

*Angel name:*

**Kilsatvavi**

To remove from the cells, the memory of traumatic creation

*Angel name:*

**22. Paarisvit-skubalva**   **Tru-esbi**

To remove the impulse to constrict from the stomach

*Angel name:*

**23. Kaarutsalvavi**   **Neshpata**

To remove fear of our vastness from the high mind

*Angel name:*

**24. Baalich-bravabu**   **Kaanish-vavet-uruha**

To create the optimum ratio of density in the body

**25. Akanavush-erespa**

**Klanek-vravu-savuta**

To dissolve bodily matrices and static patterns of obsolete reactions

**26. Pluhas-estaval**

**Nunanesh-usetvi**

To create a frame of reference between our heart
and the Infinite during our expansion

**27. Kaarachselvi-nurusta**

**Tri-eshlava**

To establish the optimum performance of the body's resources

## 28. Kursetni-uklesh

*Angel name:*

**Niklesvi**

To enhance power and energy within physical matter

## 29. El-klaresh-spi-uva

*Angel name:*

**Nisetbla-uvu**

The equal distribution of bodily resources
through the activation of inner morality

## 30. Bibavet-uselvavi

*Angel name:*

**Araspratlva**

The restoration of innocence to inner and outer senses

*Angel name:*

**31. Kurachbirat-havrusta**     **Ninachvi**

To remove illusory frequencies from the body

*Angel name:*

**32. Kaarsat-barestruha**     **Gilgal-vileshvi**

To open the unified field of the minds to Infinite Presence

**FOR ALZHEIMER'S DISORDER:**

Use sigils 1-7 plus sigils 33, 34 and 35.
The use of sigils 8 and 9 may also be of help with some exhibiting Alzheimer's.

**AUTISM:**

The same sigils can also be used for autism, plus sigils 8 and 9.

## 33. Nusta-erechvrahur

*Angel name:*

**Vilives-pahur**

For the removal of heavy metals from the brain

## 34. Kariknuspavaa

*Angel name:*

**Kurutprahe**

For the strengthening of the lymphatic system

## 35. Berek-pratlhut

*Angel name:*

**Suhuvatvata**

For the delivering of oxygen to the energy producing
organelles of brain cells

**36. Kirit-nuvech-spavi**

*Angel name:*
**Brivach-sabuta**

The removal of all discordance

**37. Kluhavech-spavi**

*Angel name:*
**Estrevananu-hash**

For the revelation of absolute truth and clarity

**38. Kaanish-serbatu**

*Angel name:*
**Unechsvi-harvuta**

For the removal of fear of survival

**39. Baarasavut-elekvi**

*Angel name:*
**Kiristrava-vilines**

For the restoration of angelic powers to man

**40. Kaalech-uvasta-sevetvi**

*Angel name:*
**Sitri-manunesh**

For the restoration of the abilities to do high magic in human DNA

**41. Paalchva-nenubush-sparura**

*Angel name:*
**Pitri-nanunet**

For the ability to work with alchemy of light in healing

### 42. Trubabesvek-keleshni

*Angel name:*

**Tru-esvi-besbi**

For the ability to work with alchemy of frequency in healing

### 43. Trabiliknis-uhastra

*Angel name:*

**Vristech-biristaa**

For the removal of patterns of emergency

### 44. Fraternuk-steveliva

*Angel name:*

**Klugava**

For harmony and full co-operation in light

*Angel name:*

## 45. Pelish-ustra-nenavish

**Klugavi-ugranot**

For the harmonious frequencies of peace

# Enlightenment Level II

## GLU-AVA-URUHIT

The angel for fluid and graceful change through
Kaanish Belvaspata Level II

**Note:** Before starting a level of Kaanish Belvaspata, look at the sigil of the angel for fluid and graceful change for that specific level. Call the name of the angel and say:

"By the power of your sigil that I hold, I call on you to create a fluid and graceful process of purification and enlightenment through level II of Kaanish Belvaspata."

**1. Kinash-setvevu-aranach**

*Angel name:*
**Stiblnesvi**

For rebirthing the self with love and respect

**2. Kunash-helesvi-spechva**

*Angel name:*
**Kininash-shelvavi**

For inspired self-parenting

**3. Ninushet-belechvi-harusta**

*Angel name:*
**Kishat-anesvi**

For the complete dissolving of the magnetic matrix
(the "pain" body)

**4. Kavavish-unesvi-servevaa**

*Angel name:*
**Mishpi-he-reva**

For the joyous re-union into Oneness

**5. Michmishet-nestu-servetut**

*Angel name:*
**Pi-iharestat**

For the reclaiming of the wholeness of self

**6. Nichtaa-uklesvi-selvuvaa**

*Angel name:*
**Keenash-heresvi**

For the flourishing of abundant life

**7. Kuchbarach-nashte-perut-haruva**

*Angel name:*
**Nistuperevu**

For the receiving of exponential insights

**8. Nuchpa-seretu-suvetvi**

*Angel name:*
**Mishivet-peres**

For complete inner peace and unconditional oneness

**9. Kunus-paresva-kinushta-uvechvi**

*Angel name:*
**Kru-anetvi-selveva**

For functioning from the fullest DNA strand capacity

## 10. Kru-avas-tranadoch-pilesha

*Angel name:*

**Uselvi-here-nat**

For self-forgiveness through compassionate understanding

## 11. Arasnusetvila-vra-ur-tra-unes

*Angel name:*

**Petri-bilebach**

For the full and equitable restoration of resources

## 12. Nus-strech-uhus-pananech

*Angel name:*

**Klihe-selvatu**

For the removal of the illusion of external geometry

**13. Kli-iheves-ubech-sta-uva**

*Angel name:*
**Nisti-bile-bach**

For the removal of the illusion of loss

**14. Mishet-ninesvu-kalisva**

*Angel name:*
**Kruve-pli-esh-narusta**

For the removal of cyclical and repetitive patterns in cosmic life

**15. Sitlhur-skaluva-neshvi**

*Angel name:*
**Paranut-uskelvi**

For the restoration of self-determination and sovereignty

**16. Brubas-natvi-skalech-piresh-haresvi**

*Angel name:*
**Klua-bak-belesvi**

For inner support and the activation and
contribution of inner well-being

**17. Kirchva-nenusv-tra-uva**

*Angel name:*
**Skalesh-bilesva**

The healing and implementation of skipped developmental stages

**18. Minesh-trekbar-selvuva**

*Angel name:*
**Nusbak-heresut**

The complete elimination of harmful experimentation

**19. Kaalchverbret-sesatchvi-kerunet**

**Pli-erek-veresta**

For the belief that progress is easily accomplished
and self-belief in our ability to succeed

**20. Kunash-petruvi-haresva**

**Kelsetvi-varuha**

For the removal of memory blocks of that which is

**21. Parash-urek-sevuvi**

**Trinesvi-arurat**

For the removal of memories of that which is not

## 22. Kinesh-paravi

*Angel name:*
**Kersvi-eru-nat**

For the removal of all forms of dictatorships

## 23. Stubaru-eretvi

*Angel name:*
**Kluvas-pi-retvi**

For the balancing of all stagnation, atrophy and hyper-activity

## 24. Nunash-erklat-vrabish

*Angel name:*
**Ninsur-per-het-varesva**

For the full ability to have and interpret all perspectives

**25. Kerich-verna-servatu**

*Angel name:*

**Keenash-vitvi**

For reclaiming Sovereignty of effective expression

**26. Plubesh-estavi-nes-habasta**

*Angel name:*

**Pirhut-pratlvi**

For establishing a relationship with impeccable power

**27. Kaaru-selvi-ubesvi**

*Angel name:*

**Kuras-stret-vi**

For healing feelings of abandonment by power

**28. Kerash-prehu-satva-unash**

*Angel name:*
**Krikenet-uluhur**

For trust in Infinite Guidance and being heard

---

**29. Mishtave-piranukvi**

*Angel name:*
**Stuchva-subavet**

For the removal of the illusion of fatigue

---

**30. Virsat-eleklu-vileshvi**

*Angel name:*
**Nachsta-minuvir**

For perpetual self-regeneration and rejuvenation

**31. Mishpa-heruhit-ustatvi**

**Kinashvet-ruvi**

For removing all psychological bondage from expectations

**32. Kaaresh-steravu-kinachvi**

*Angel name:*
**Pla-ater-brubashvi**

For removing all compensatory behavior patterns

**33. Kaarsbak-stetvaa-uvaster**

*Angel name:*
**Kluhuva-eresbi**

For complete trust in the perfection of the One Life

# Enlightenment Level III

## PAARABUSH-HERSEVAT

The angel for fluid and graceful change through
Kaanish Belvaspata Level III

**Note:** Before starting a level of Kaanish Belvaspata, look at the sigil
of the angel for fluid and graceful change for that specific level. Call
the name of the angel and say:

"By the power of your sigil that I hold, I call on you to create
a fluid and graceful process of purification and enlightenment through level III of Kaanish Belvaspata."

**1. Erech-tranavich-hurespa**

*Angel name:*
**Kirivabesbi**

For the complete dissolving of the illusion of space

**2. Birispak-unesvi-haras-stat**

*Angel name:*
**Estava-bireshbi**

For the complete dissolving of duality

**3. Kinavi-selvavu-urasbi**

*Angel name:*
**Kluhava-ste-vavi**

For the complete dissolving of polarity

**4. Kelvabi-estabi-minuvach**

*Angel name:*
**Nechstach-va-vi-hereshva**

For the complete dissolving of the four illusions of light[1]

**5. Klubaset-neshbahur**

*Angel name:*
**Pitri-balusva-hereshvi**

For the complete dissolving of the illusions of sound
(the echo and the soundless vacuum)

**6. Nichtu-servatet**

*Angel name:*
**Kilesti-haruvar**

For the complete assimilation of potential

---

1 **Note**: The four illusions of light are the mirror, the rainbow (the refraction of light), the mirage and the lens (also the fractured kaleidoscope lens). See Almine's online course, the first month of Academy of Alchemy — Tools of Illumination

**7. Pelesh-vrihar-salvustet**

*Angel name:*
**Nunesh-urechsti**

For the elimination of the wisdom of past experience

**8. Biritbek-giritna-selvavu**

*Angel name:*
**Pruvetsklaba**

For the complete elimination of separation
in the chambers and strands of DNA

**9. Nuchter-servu-eleshar**

*Angel name:*
**Glaneeshservatu**

For the formation of a unified DNA field

**10. Nusba-erestu-klanivespa**

*Angel name:*
**Palech-nenestu**

For the elimination of traditional and racial templates in soul-force[2]

---

**11. Kluvirit-stachvavi-nesva**

*Angel name:*
**Uvabechspi**

For the dissolving of the illusion of separation and
existence of the building blocks of life

---

**12. Bli-esh-uret-plihek-ustava**

*Angel name:*
**Minavech-spereru**

For the dissolving of the illusion of accomplishments of the dream

---

2 **Note:** For further explanations of these concepts, see Almine's online course of the first
month of *Academy of Alchemy — Tools of Illumination*

**13. Niklesh-baruchspi**

*Angel name:*
**Kluvechsbi-arurash**

For the elimination of the illusion of the
existence of external information

**14. Keenash-virabak**

*Angel name:*
**Nuchsperaa**

For the removal of the belief system of unfair stress of life
causing failure of life-forms to live their highest potential

**15. Unech-vribesh-erenut**

*Angel name:*
**Kilinesvabek**

For the removal of the belief that the Infinite loves conditionally
and punishes if we don't meet expectations

## 16. Klanavish-steravu

*Angel name:*

**Nuchstavru-skelavich**

For the removal of the belief that we are imperfectly made, causing us to suffer or not live up to the highest potential

## 17. Kaanek-vishvabaa-erurek

*Angel name:*

**Nichtu-ser-vavu**

For the removal of the belief that Creation is based on trial and error

## 18. Kenuva-pirithur-selvuva-vechbi

*Angel name:*

**Kelsit-heresba**

For the removal of the belief that the purpose of Creation is so that the Infinite might learn about Its own existence

**19. Nuchtavu-skelesva**

**Unesbi-skala-lot**

For the removal of the belief that we should have
more abilities at any specific moments

**20. Kisahur-pilit-vribach-eruvi**

**Kilich-birit-verbaa**

For the removal of the belief that any flaw in
the timing of manifestation can exist

# Enlightenment Level IV

## PILISH-HERSET-VARUKLA

The angel for fluid and graceful change through
Kaanish Belvaspata Level IV

**Note:** Before starting a level of Kaanish Belvaspata, look at the sigil
of the angel for fluid and graceful change for that specific level. Call
the name of the angel and say:

"By the power of your sigil that I hold, I call on you to create
a fluid and graceful process of purification and enlightenment through level IV of Kaanish Belvaspata."

*Angel name:*

**1. Kiris-barabak-ustanve-mishet** **Kiristat-ve**

For the removal of the belief that unfairness and inequity can exist

---

*Angel name:*

**2. Kilikhur-subatve** **Erestahutvi**

For the removal of the belief that the Infinite exploits
and uses us for Its own purpose

---

*Angel name:*

**3. Paarish-bravek-salvuvet-anish** **Klugvaba-ineshvi**

For the removal of the belief that the Cosmos is run in an inept
way or that there is something the Infinite does not know

**4. Kaalistar-urvavi-unachsvi**

**Kurunut-stelvavi**

For the removal of the illusion of the Infinite
measuring us by unfair standards

**5. Mishtel-blavuch-steravi**

*Angel name:*
**Unashvi-heresta**

For the removal of the illusion of the Infinite
requiring us to grow at an unfair pace

**6. Nishtar-blahep-ustava-kanunish**

*Angel name:*
**Silvevi-erestar-nachvi**

For the removal of the illusion of the responsibility
placed upon us being too heavy

**7. Kelech-vibrish-harnustat**

*Angel name:*
**Nichstor-balashvi**

For the removal of the illusion that Cosmic Life is a tyrannical system that does not allow for self-expression

**8. Aralesh-mispi**

*Angel name:*
**Ku-uhuret-spavi**

For the removal of the illusion that the Infinite has unrealistic expectations of us

**9. Kaaratvi-uranesh-staruvi**

*Angel name:*
**Karas-uvra-hespi**

For the removal of the illusion that Cosmic Life blocks us, rather than promoting our flourishing

**10. Pelespravi-usetvi**

*Angel name:*
**Kiritna-uhelesh-bi**

For the removal of the illusion that life is
to be endured rather than enjoyed

**11. Kaalichba-ninustreva-piritvi**

*Angel name:*
**Gaalech-pritvaa**

For the removal of fear of failure through inadequacy

**12. Kubalva-utrechvi-staruva**

*Angel name:*
**Stubaret-unurasvi**

For the removal of fear of missing what we should know or do

**13. Kaanish-mechspa-meruhit**

*Angel name:*
**Kalsva-erut-trahe**

For the removal of the fear of not seeing
and making the right choice

**14. Kulchba-merurit-skalvava**

*Angel name:*
**Kuranat-valshpi**

The removal of the illusion that we can
be separated from what we love

**15. Ustret-bileshba-astavu**

*Angel name:*
**Estre-mirash-piravit**

For removal of the feeling that we are misplaced;
that we can be anywhere we don't belong

*Angel name:*

**16. Kunish-pretpraha-usitveresva    Nukvi-ster-avet**

For the removal of the illusion that we
have an end to our journey of life

*Angel name:*

**17. Skalikvich-suvavetvi    Kilash-pratu-var**

For the removal of feeling as though we are in a state
of emergency because bad things may happen

*Angel name:*

**18. Brubasput-uknachbi    Kiritnasv-uravet**

For the removal of the illusion that home is an external place

**19. Heretprabush-pravaa**

**Usalvavi-knichva**

For the removal of the illusion of feeling our
unique gifts are not valued nor understood

**20. Kaa-avubrit-pelish-vabraa**

**Kaanish-veles-bra**

For the removal of the feeling of being unprotected against harm

# Enlightenment Level V

## KUNASH-BIRUSHVA

The angel for fluid and graceful change through
Kaanish Belvaspata Level V

**Note:** Before starting a level of Kaanish Belvaspata, look at the sigil of the angel for fluid and graceful change for that specific level. Call the name of the angel and say:

"By the power of your sigil that I hold, I call on you to create a fluid and graceful process of purification and enlightenment through level V of Kaanish Belvaspata."

**1. Nustechvi-velebra-hasvi**

*Angel name:*
**Kalabi-suvavet**

For the attitude of surrendering to the moment

---

**2. Eretkle-uhurabish**

*Angel name:*
**Selvavi-pireshnuravet**

For the attitude of taking full responsibility for the environment

---

**3. Keenasat-plubakvi-erutprave**

*Angel name:*
**Kelsut-manavech**

For the surrendering to inner guidance

**4.  Graanik-spelebaa-skechvi**

*Angel name:*
**Vilshkrabi-minhursat**

For the complete wholeness of self through the
implementation of the 144 self-wheels[3]

**5.  Kilinat-esvavi-nusba**

*Angel name:*
**Grunik-ustatvi**

For inner contentment and peace through
embodying the 4 Wheels of Inner Peace[4]

**6.  Selva-nusvi-sklaurach-uhelasvi**

*Angel name:*
**Pitirach-ushel-vi**

For the embodying of the 13 Wheels of the Manifestation of Majesty[5]

---

3  See the section on 144 self-wheels
4  See the section on the 4 Wheels of Inner Peace
5  See the section on the 13 wheels of the Manifestation of Majesty

# THE ONE THAT CONTAINS ALL

## THE WHEEL OF THE GOD KINGDOM'S SIGILS[6]

*Angel name:*

### 7. Kenesh-pararuknichverti-uselvaa

### Stuvabechsbinusurubach

For the complete synchronization of our environment
with the perfection of our individuation.
Let me embody the Wheel That Contains All[7].

---

6 For further information on the god-kingdom, see *Secrets of the Hidden Realms* (The Evolutionary Stages of Man)
7 See the One Wheel that Contains All

# Closing Sigils for a Session or Initiation

Praise

Love

Gratitude

# BOOK TWO

# The 144 Self Wheels

# The Use of Wheels

A wheel is a visual image conveying non-cognitive, sacred and empowering information. Wheels are similar to gateways through which specific healing frequencies are drawn and are power sources in the same way a holy object would be. Accessed through the heart, we allow their beneficial influences into our lives. Wheels used in sequence build upon each other and tell a story. The Self Wheels can be visualized as if standing on a disc, moving from the bottom of the feet to the top of the head and the Lahun chakra, either singly or in sequence.

Wheels may have specific directions such as **The 144 Self-Wheels of the Source of Life**[8]. The 144 Self Wheels within this manual can be found on the Ascension Angels and Astrology of Isis websites; see these sites for detailed instructions:

- www.ascensionangels.com under "Self-Wheels and their Angels"
- www.astrology-of-isis.com under "The 144 Self-Wheels of the Source of Life"

## POSSIBLE USES

- Wheels can be placed on the walls of a healing space.
- Wheels can be placed directly in or on an afflicted area of the body.
- Specific wheels can be placed under a healing table when working on someone.
- Wheels can be taped unseen under chairs where you spend a lot of time or under your bed.
- Have a wheel made up as a pendant to wear around your neck.

8 See www.astrology-of-isis.com

## Wheel of Adoration of the Infinite Mother and Father

1

## Wheel of Highly Refined Frequency and Light

2

## Wheel of Ultimate Refinement of Life

3

## Wheel of Passionate Exploration

4

## Wheel of Self-Exploration

5

## Wheel of Gratification in Beingness

6

## Wheel of Self-Courage

7

## Wheel of Self-Sufficiency

8

## Wheel of Self-Knowledge

9

## Wheel of Self-Gratitude

10

## Wheel of Self-Praise

11

## Wheel of Self-Celebration

12

## Wheel of Self-Beauty

13

## Wheel of Self-Grace

14

## Wheel of Self-Sustenance

15

## Wheel of Integrated Oneness

16

## Wheel of Fire Within

17

## Wheel of Self-Truth

18

## Wheel of Self-Trust

19

## Wheel of Self-Generated Resource

20

## Wheel of Entrained Frequency

21

## Wheel of Innocence

22

## Wheel of Purity

23

## Wheel of Adoration in Action

24

# Wheel of Regeneration

25

# Wheel of Self-Respect

26

## Wheel of Self-Directed Desire of the Heart

27

## Wheel of Joy in Creation

28

## Wheel of Self-Mastery in Action

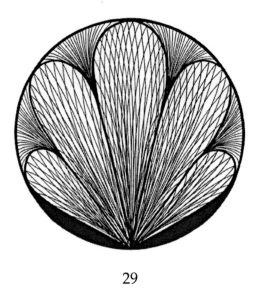

29

## Wheel of Self-Seeing Perfection

30

## Wheel of Compassionate Understanding

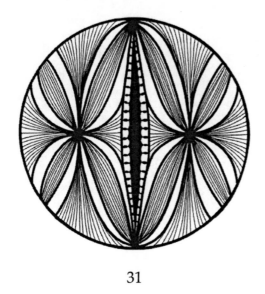

31

## Wheel of Self-Confidence

32

## Wheel of Self-Acceptance

33

## Wheel of Clarity

34

## Wheel of Self-Belief

35

## Wheel of Self-Determination

36

# Wheel of Interconnectedness

37

# Wheel of Self-Motivation

38

## Wheel of Pristine Co-existence with Nature

39

## Wheel of Self-Accomplishment

40

## Wheel of Self-Love in Doingness

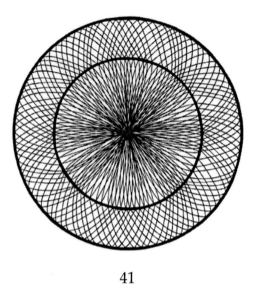

41

## Wheel of Self-Light in Beingness

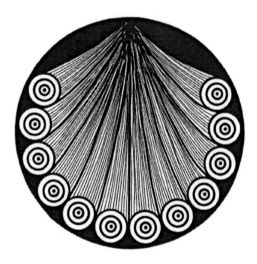

42

## Wheel of Self-Perception

43

## Wheel of Unlimited Access to Knowledge

44

# Wheel of Experiential Knowledge

45

# Wheel of Self-Dignity

46

## Wheel of Fluidity in Mastery

47

## Wheel of Self-Discovery

48

## Wheel of Devoted Service to Infinite Mother and Father

49

## Wheel of Appreciation of Self-Perfection

50

## Wheel of Appreciating Self in External Beauty

51

## Wheel of Plentiful Supply

52

## Wheel of Appreciating Beauty

53

## Wheel of Self-Guidance

54

## Wheel of Self-Acknowledgement

55

## Wheel of Self-Generated Focus in Life

56

## Wheel of Peaceful Desires of Heart

57

## Wheel of Balance in Motion

58

## Wheel of Alliances with Infinite Intent

59

## Wheel of Self-Appreciation

60

# Wheel of Self-Responsibility

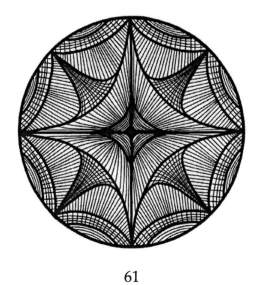

61

# Wheel of Self-Reliance

62

## Wheel of Acknowledging Self-Contributions

63

## Wheel of Seeing the Value of All Life

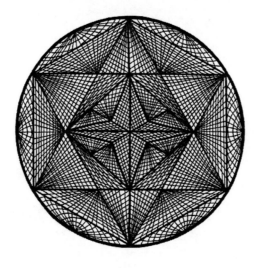

64

## Wheel of Unified Fields

65

## Wheel of Exponential Growth

66

## Wheel of Self-Awareness

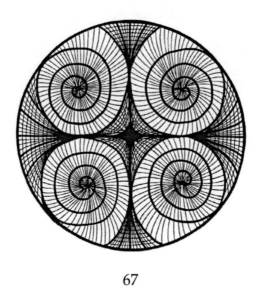

67

## Wheel of Birthing New Paradigms

68

## Wheel of Self-Empowerment

69

## Wheel of Purification through Gratitude

70

## Wheel of Luminous Living

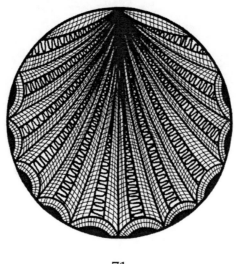

71

## Wheel of Self-Recognition of Uniqueness

72

## Wheel of Integrated Sub-personalities

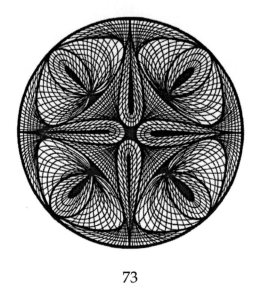

73

## Wheel of Embracing Life

74

## Wheel of Inclusiveness

75

## Wheel of Self-Purity

76

## Wheel of Enthusiastic Surrender to the Now

77

## Wheel of Self-Nurturing

78

## Wheel of Self-Stability through Faith

79

## Wheel of Self-Assurance through Humility

80

# Wheel of Listening with the Heart

81

# Wheel of Delighted Self-Expression

82

## Wheel of Self-Encouragement

83

## Wheel of Moving Horizons

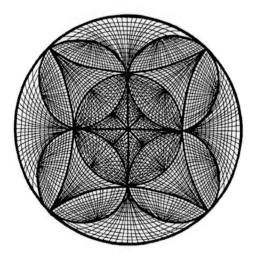

84

## Wheel of Cooperative Endeavors

85

## Wheel of Communion with Nature

86

## Wheel of Exploration of Self through Others

87

## Wheel of Acknowledging of Self-Divinity

88

# Wheel of Interpretive Dance

89

# Wheel of Appreciative Awareness of Details

90

## Wheel of Efficient Use of Resources

91

## Wheel of Humble Assimilation of New Potential

92

## Wheel of Countless Achievements

93

## Wheel of Expanded Aspirations

94

## Wheel of Deepening Experiences

95

## Wheel of Fluidly Shifting Consciousness

96

# Wheel of Self-Wisdom

97

# Wheel of Self-Assessment

98

## Wheel of Simplicity of Choices

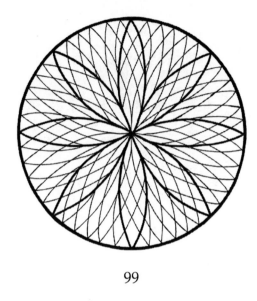

99

## Wheel of Freedom from Nostalgia of the Past

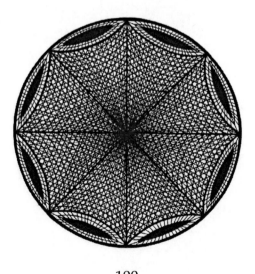

100

## Wheel of Collaboration to Do Life-Enhancing Work

101

## Wheel of Creating New Memories

102

## Wheel of Boundless Growth through Grace

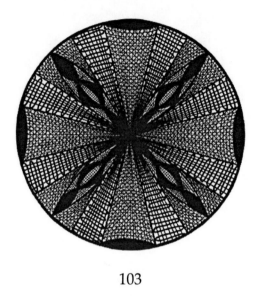

103

## Wheel of Individual Relationship

104

## Wheel of Abundant Living

105

## Wheel of Joyful Journey of Discovery

106

## Wheel of Emotional Self-Fulfillment

107

## Wheel of New Creations

108

# Wheel of all-Encompassing Presence

109

# Wheel of Releasing Duty

110

## Wheel of Releasing Resistance

111

## Wheel of Authenticity

112

## Wheel of Self-Manifested Intent

113

## Wheel of One Heart-Mind

114

## Wheel of Pristine Creations

115

## Wheel of Imaginative Expression

116

## Wheel of Expanding Inner Sight

117

## Wheel of Heaven on Earth

118

## Wheel of Acknowledging Earth's Divinity

119

## Wheel of Communion with the Infinite

120

## Wheel of Complete Release

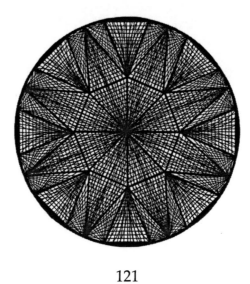

121

## Wheel of Deeper Understanding of the Infinite

122

## Wheel of Dissolving Obsolete Patterns

123

## Wheel of Unlimited Learning

124

## Wheel of Dissolving Dysfunctionality

125

## Wheel of Complete Trust in Divine Order

126

## Wheel of Flowering

127

## Wheel of Honoring Diversity

128

## Wheel of Oneness with the Infinite

129

## Wheel of Full Emotional Expression

130

## Wheel of Eternal Life

131

## Wheel of Creating Sacred Space

132

## Wheel of Physical Manifestation

133

## Wheel of Restoration to Magical Life

134

## Wheel of Mastery of Alchemy

135

## Wheel of Becoming Divine Architects

136

## Wheel of Instant Access to Infinite Knowledge

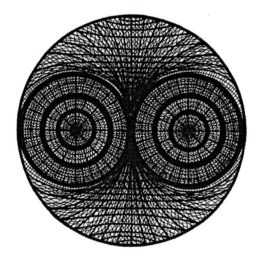

137

## Wheel of Restoration of Magical Kingdoms

138

## Wheel of Dissolving Stagnant Boundaries

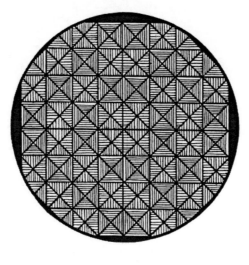

139

## Wheel of Dissolving Programming

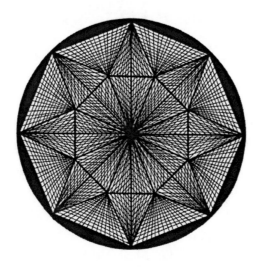

140

## Wheel of Perfect Harmony

141

## Wheel of Limitless Creativity

142

## Wheel of Unobstructed Vision

143

## Wheel of Everlasting Guidance by the Infinite

144

# The 144 Self Wheels

## PART 1

During the Dublin workshop in November 2008 the 144 self wheels (drawn by Eva from Toronto, Canada) were introduced to us by Almine. Each person present was to select a wheel for themselves. This wheel was changed by Mother/Infinite through Almine. If the wheel chosen by the student was not the most appropriate wheel for them. In other words if the wheel was not in line with the gift that the Infinite wished for the student; one that would bring new consciousness or awareness to them of who they really are. Through Almine, the Infinite then spoke to the group gathered and gave a full account of the wheel for each person present, including the benefits the wheel would bring to each of their lives and the benefits the wheels would be to the entire cosmos.

## PART 2

One of the tasks Almine asked of the group was for each student to take three wheels and to contemplate on each wheel for a period of time and then share with the group what the wheels meant to the student. Part two of this document is the sharing of each student's understanding of the wheels they contemplated on.

## COMMENTS FROM ALMINE ON THE SELF-WHEELS

(Almine gave each student a blessing during the time the students were relating their understanding of the wheels.) Almine speaks to the students: The blessing I am going to be doing has a very specific purpose. Its purpose is to help you remember. We are going to be doing that today.

My brothers and sisters, it is about remembering those first few moments when life flowed through us. That is what my blessing is about and as you speak about the wheels, the language is going to help fellow classmates remember who they are.

Let's take Rie's wheel, for instance. I just want to show you how nothing can be taken for granted and why you cannot take these wheels at their superficial value. Her wheel is the efficient use of resources. On the surface it sounds like she is good at using money. It doesn't mean that at all. The resources we are talking about are those of consciousness. That is that what we are made of, the energy, the power of the cosmos. We have given you some key notes about being a master. One of them is fluidity and the other is the knowing that you know nothing. One of the others is the efficient use of cosmic resources.

For years before Mother called me to do this work, as a Nagual I was training apprentices in the Toltec way. One of the key Nagual tenets I taught is that you live frugally. In other words you don't waste a single resource because one of the cosmic resources that flow through you is mastery. So the wheel will unfold itself to you. As we learn to work with them they will reveal the ways of accessing their power. Understanding them is another story. Really contemplate layer upon layer, upon layer, upon layer as they are multiple layers deep.

During the break I was seeing your wheels. My brothers and sisters, I would see your wheels but there would be a wheel behind a wheel, behind a wheel. Those are our conceptions of these principles that they stand for. They are not what they seem. So treat them with great humility and respect.

Helge once told us a story. He received a sigil from Mother that looked like a Belvaspata sigil. The masters here in Ireland each got their own sigil, which is like their own power object. He is a chemistry teacher and he had some students in his class who really just didn't want to learn. They were disruptive. He took his sigil to his work. The disruptive students left and he was left with the real students who wanted to learn and his life became easier.

These wheels are beyond those sigils you received and those sigils were so powerful. Our sister Joanne put her sigil into a photocopier and it wouldn't copy. She put it through her fax machine to see if she could get a copy and it wouldn't work. Finally she scanned it with her computer but the computer printout ran to over one thousand pages of computer language. The information it contained was so powerful. The whole body of cosmic resources comes through these wheels. Why? They were made through these wheels. So I just wanted to tell you I could see who you were by looking at your wheels. I was almost in tears back there as I was working with you and your individual wheels. They are your lenses my brothers and sisters. It is so exquisite.

# Almine Provides Mother's Explanations of the Wheels

**Wheel 2: Highly Refined Frequency (for Marian).**

Mother says the patterns within you have been removed and now you can make any pattern you like. See the wheel as another form of a template. The old one was another form of artificial intelligence, another form of disempowering. This is your pattern. She is shining Her light through it. It is crystal clear. I am looking at it and there is no lens, just a crystal clear beam and Her light shines through the beam. The pattern that you make from it is up to you. Mother says she needs to explain to you what it now means, that it is not a pattern within you. Mother says it is the song that is given to you as a gift. This is a song She has gifted to you. She says this song I sing for you, My daughter, is my gift to you. The refined light and frequency that is carried upon the notes of My song is that of which I am made. In giving you this song you are given a part of My being to access. Your life shall open from it and great joy shall flood your way. May you see it My daughter.

**Wheel 6: Wheel of Gratification in Beingness (for Carmel).**

The song that you have has been carried with you from ancient times. The gratification in beingness is a song not that I give you but one you have always given creation. Well done, My daughter. You have fulfilled such a destiny, for in times of great discomfort when a nightmare plagued My soul you brought forth gratification in beingness. It is in understanding the imperfect creations that were and the death that came to them, that true gratification in living can take place. It came through My daughter Constance two or three Pods ago, posed as the question, What is the value of life? We can only know that when we know that it (life) can be taken away. The deep meaningful living, the gratification is in little things as well as the big picture.

**Wheel 7: Wheel of Self Courage (for Kay).**
Mother says that it is in holding fast to the knowledge that purity must conquer all, for it is all and it has never been otherwise, that self courage is born. Self doubt comes from believing the upside down mirrors that used to be, that tells us that in some way that we are of lesser value. Self courage comes from piercing through the appearances and seeing that which is and that which shall always prevail. As life is lived in purity and innocence, courage is there for it is aligned with that which eternally shall reign. That will take a lot of time for you to figure that out but talk to Joe to figure out ways that you can get this.

**Wheel 13: Wheel of Self Beauty (for Joe).**
You have found beauty all around you, yet have not stopped to see it in yourself. You have found beauty in that which you have seen in the Infinite's face, but you have valued yourself at times, My son, by what you do. The beauty in you is more than a thousand suns rising. Oh dear, this is not going to be easy, I don't know how you folks keep dry eyes through this (Almine). It is like wild horses running free across the fields. It is as magnificent as the dawn and you have been a light bearer like he who carries the starry skies for the other masters here in this land. Is that not self beauty?

**Wheel 15: Wheel of Self Sustenance (for Elizabeth from Ireland).**
The song that I give you, My daughter, is that you might remember that I have placed everything within you. That I have placed within you the gentleness of the rabbit who makes a lair for her little ones, that I have placed within you the boundless strength of a thousand

earthquakes, that I have placed within you the beauty of the sun and the stars and the earth dancing together. All that I am is within you. It is therefore fitting that the self is fully self sustaining. This song is the memory of all that you are.

**Wheel 17: Wheel of the Fire Within (for Rose).**
The fire within is a discovery of the journey. It is that which leads you on and the song will lead you out of boundaries that have been, and the song will lead you to see through the cardboard walls of man's sub-creations. For the fire within is not contained by appearances. It does not take face value as an answer. The fire within will find absolute truth.

**Wheel 19: Wheel of Self Trust (for Sheila).**
Self trust, My daughter, is born of self love and the self love is born of self knowledge. It has been aptly said this day to always seek to understand the self but to remember that you never can. So Mother says that it is in knowing the self that self loves comes. Where there is self love there is self trust. The self knowledge can be felt by seeing Me in all that is around you. For all perception is really self-perception. For that which I am you are also and that which is around you but mirrors your beauty. However 'mirrors' is not the right word – it *shows* your beauty. Thus let trust be there. I shall never let you falter.

**Wheel 23: Wheel of Purity (for Gaby).**
In dark places have you walked, beloved son, and you have thought that it could taint you. But it never could. For as a lily that grows in the mud, purity has always been there and you have brought light into dark places. I will fill your heart with My purity this day and the fulfillment that you seek will be within. The song of this gift that I give you is a wheel of combined purified frequency and light. Each

wheel is that, reminding you that you are the pure place where ever you are.

### Wheel 24: Wheel of Adoration in Action (for Niels).

Mother says that you have chosen this. She did not give you this because She wanted to see which one you would choose. Mother says you have chosen that, which is the song of all life, that the song that all life sings at this time is "Adoration in Action" and this you have aligned yourself with and this will bring great power in your life. For all that you align yourself with, which represents portions of the Infinite's being within these wheels is power.

### Wheel 25: Wheel of Regeneration (for Siobhan).

When the flames ignited the masculine planets and the flowers ignited the feminine planets it was so that restructuring and destructuring were heightened, but they joined as one. Regeneration became a way of life. You will be regenerated. Know it faithfully in your heart. Speak not words that are to the contrary and you will youthen (grow younger) and through you many will be led to do the same. Regeneration is the perfect balancing of that which is receptive and proactive within. This gift I give you this day, My daughter.

### Wheel 27: Wheel of Self Directed Desire of the Heart (for Denis).

Mother says, "Don't look back", for in your absence* life just survives but now your heart will lead you and it will bring you and your beloved safely home. The future will unfold before you and your heart will tell you at all times which direction it is you should take even if it makes no sense to others who cannot hear the song of self-directed motivation from the heart. She has said that much had been taken from you. Mother is saying to me now that Janet also was taken (*to another cosmos as explained to us by Almine) and most certainly people in your environment over the last year would have sensed that. But Mother wanted you to know that. So to My brother (Ben, Denis's partner) Mother is saying that from you, much was taken and a sacrifice was made to keep a cosmos alive that had to be alive. Much will be given. Be at peace and your hearts will guide you.

## Wheel 28: Wheel of Joy in Creation (for Annette).

Mother gives you a gift that at this time has not yet been activated amongst this group but it will be. However it is enhanced in you. Through the art that you do, purity will be restored to those who live in Europe and eventually to all the earth. You will draw the mandalas of life and I will speak them in your ear and you, My daughter, will hear. As you draw them, all creation will be cleared. It is the joy in creation that will break the drudgery of work that is mindlessly done. In other words people will start to feel joy in their work by doing it creatively.

## Wheel 34: Wheel of Clarity (for Ellen).

I could not believe that they did not take you to the other cosmos. They took the leadership of this place which you certainly are part of. I kept asking "what about Ellen, what about Ellen?" Mother is saying now the explanation will come.

Just like Carmel, this is not a new song for you. The song of clarity you have always sung. In your case it is the song of seeing clearly. It has always been constant, that which brings clarity to others. You bring clarity to a situation. Mother is saying that you have always known what the highest road is and what the lowest road is. You always choose the highest. Mother is saying that through the ages you have been like a light beacon even in the darkest times of dreaming and she is saying thank you. So this is your song my sister.

## Wheel 48: Wheel of Self Discovery (for Helena).

It is time for self-discovery to take place. It has been disconcerting for you have stepped out of boundaries that you thought you never would. But it is the time that you find the purity of your heart lies untainted and does not lie within the belief systems imposed upon you. Mother says She is giving you this song at this time in your life because it time for stepping out of the boxes of your life. She says you are doing it on behalf of the people that are not of Poland but of the Caucasus Mountains - Mother says the Ukrainian and Caucasian areas.

I am seeing a map and there are mountains and there is something that lies to the east of the mountains. She is saying that region, I don't know if it is the Ukraine, but She is saying in that region the people are in boxes and they don't step out of them in case someone in the village or town would speak about them. They don't dare show themselves. She says you have taken the boxes on in your life to overthrow this. She says that particular region of earth is the acupuncture point of new beginnings and it has stagnation. You have done this as a service. Enough! So this is over. The wheel is given. You can step free and step free in your mind. It doesn't mean you have to change your life, Helena. It is in your mind. I don't know what it means because I can see you want to ask me that. You ask the wheel. It will reveal it to you.

## Wheel 49: Wheel of Devoted Service to the Infinite Mother and Father (for Cory).

Mother says that this is a calling because you will be working with them inside the inner circle of the Holy City. She says it is a calling that begins with the people in the street. As you see Mother in your brothers and sisters and in service, you serve Her. It will be that you shall be, not in the very distant future, (Almine: I don't know what that means to Mother but it is very encouraging) in the city itself.

It is the time for the full passion of your being to come out and as you do such service, which is that which takes the place of work, it will be done with passion everywhere for you embody its frequency. There is a lot there and it is very deep. You are going to have to contemplate it.

**Wheel 52: Wheel of Plentiful Supply (for Anne Mundell).**
This is your archetypal role and for those that are here present, humanity's archetypal roles are over. It is very hard work. These are not Mother's words, they are mine. It's very hard work to be an archetype because you carry weight that isn't even yours. Mother says the plentiful supply is for you, not through you to others. There are remnants being shoved down today. Let's take a look at it. Helena has been an archetype for people who have boxed themselves into duty - should, could. She is stepping out of it – end of story. She doesn't represent them anymore, thank you very much. When Mother says as you do your service with passion and your passion awakens, people will get passion everywhere. It is not that she is an archetype. It is not that if she doesn't do it things will fall apart. It is simply that all of you have an influence even when you are no longer an archetype. It means you don't have to carry other people's problems around. So Mother is very specific that this gift of plentiful supply is for Anne to enjoy. It is the plentiful supply of the joy of adventure, of great satisfaction, of beingness and great exploration and abundant supply.

**Wheel 56: Wheel of Self Generated Focus in Life (for Maureen).**
When focus is not self centered there cannot be a simultaneous seeing of the big picture and the details. There are those who see the big picture but do not know how to accomplish it because they cannot see the steps that it takes. Most of humanity, because of their vision, see only the steps in front of them. But you see both - wrong

word- Mother says you will see all the perspectives at once. It is a gift of the Infinite because the Mother sees the big picture. She sees the little thing. She sees the in-between. What is the next stage? She sees all of it and She sees where everything can fluidly change. So you have this vision and She says that it is important that you are aware that you are going to be seeing things differently. Normally you would see what is on your agenda for the day. You will also see what that day is to accomplish. What it is you wish to do with the whole day. You will see how the day fits into the month. Mother says it is your choice of how big you go and when you do self generated on the details. So in other words you can go as large as you go. My sister this is seership. Because this is what a seer does. They see the whole big picture and they see how the little spot fits into the big picture. So She is basically giving you the wheel of the seer.

**Wheel 62: Wheel of Self Reliance (for Ann Fuller).**
This day let the song of self reliance be given to all beings in the cosmos. But in you it shall have a special flavor of nuanced emphasis. The sacred information that this evening will be revealed to the one who speaks (that is Almine), you shall flourish and thrive at. Mother says you will be very good at this power of the first born. The wheels function as a lens to the infinite creation within and you will see there all that is. This vision will become a part of your perspective as you walk as a goddess upon the earth. Let all humanity receive self-reliance for if they do, their relationships will no longer be in pain. The greatest challenge for humankind is to love without pain.

Pain only comes where there are attached outcomes at being loved back. Every love that we feel shakes loose cobwebs inside and sometimes it is the sole purpose for which it came by, just for a brief moment, for a week, for a month. Then it shakes loose the cobwebs. We must keep that awareness and move forward. Then another comes along that lights a lamp and again our inner landscape is enriched. Self-reliance in all beings brings about self-sovereignty and therefore joy in relationships. Mother says She has put notes in your song that allow you to throw off concerns about how others appraise you. It is not being self-referring for approval but it is more than that. Mother is saying you will become free of it, which is total self reliance where you live from self directed heart energy and not look left or right. Mother says She has made provisions so your friends should not expect you to be the same after this. Who knows, Ann might start wearing red stilettos.

## Wheel 64: Wheel of Seeing the Value of All Life (for Gregory).

Mother says you knew that one would be yours, My son. She says it is necessary to make more complete within you the beauty of the godhood that you hold. It is not that you have not seen the life, the value of life in every creature. It is that you have not valued your own as much. The same frequency that has been placed in the self-reliance wheel of My sister Ann is placed within yours as well. It is that which sees the value of your godhood and the vastness of that which you are whether others do or not. Mother is saying that in the dream there were very many negative mirrors around you as to your value. Now you will be in full awakening. Ignore the sub-creation. It is not real and it will soon dissipate like mist before the morning sun. See the value of the life the way you do but know that it is a reflection of you.

## Wheel 69: Wheel of Self Empowerment (for Angela).

Much have you hidden, goddess of light. Now it will no longer be hidden from those who are like you. Speak from the heart and from the power of your throat. Let the breath in your lungs return. (Almine's comment - let me ask Mother what She means by this). Mother says that you have not breathed deeply enough. She says that you will soon enter immortality and you will not need to breathe at all but that should be a choice. The breathing is because you could not express. The lungs have to do with self-expression. She said your breath has been shallow because you could not self-express. You were hemmed in by these who could not see. As one of the oracles among my pillars, your self-empowerment comes by emptying out all you thought you knew and radiant beauty will shine forth from you in power and in glory as is befitting a daughter who is a goddess in the temple

## Wheel 85: Wheel of Co-Operative Endeavors (for Elisabeth from Germany).

Mother says that this event has been a turning point in walking away from that which has been contrary to who you are. It was done on purpose because you clung to that which was not worthy. It was because of your speaking to me that we were reminded this week about the backward mirrors. No longer; let the grandeur shine forth. Have you not wondered why it is, so that you cannot make a mistake? I will repeat that - Why it is that you cannot make a mistake? Mother is getting ready to tell us. It is because of total cooperation with the river of life. So even when it seemed you were making a mistake you did it to be able to rectify, to perfect, to refine that which the Infinite Mother is, to refine Her Creation and Her Being. Even if it looks as thought we have made a mistake the Infinite Mother is saying it was to help refine the creations, not Her Being as She that is Pure Refinement. She says that time of your life when you had a mirror - archetypically something that had to be refined – it's over. She says that from this point on this little shackle that nevertheless was part of the co-operative endeavor with the Infinite Being is gone. There will be directness of the heart and you will shine forth. Stand forth and unfold your wings of light. No longer will you seek for crumbs, for that which is to come is great and glorious. Arise, Goddess that is the pillar of my temple! (Almine's comment - That is also one of those seriously deep ones that we are going to have to ponder.)

**Wheel 89: Wheel of Interpretive Dance (for Margaret).**
Mother is saying you will live where life is new. It is your choice. The song in the wheel that you hold and the new light that it will pour forth into your life will shake free the old ruts, for ruts are of death. The dance of interpretive potential – the interpretive dance of potential is the dance of life. Mother is giving you a very deep esoteric principal that I am very happy to know. Mother is saying that as long as new potential continually flows into any being there cannot be death. Death is the cutting off of new potential. In other words it is a stagnant pond with no pipe that feeds fresh water into it. Mother is saying that the pond will ultimately stagnate; life in it won't be able to make it if fresh water doesn't come in. Mother is saying that you have chosen the dance of life and there will be new coming through you. It is necessary that you are very aware of the instinctual guidance within and that you take time to listen. Even if you set your clock to twenty minutes earlier in the morning or twenty minutes later to bed. Just listen. Where you are listening is inside. What is it I feel like doing? I feel like taking my nightgown off and running around outside in the rain. That is not what I do but what is coming through me, because whatever it is, that is your next step of potential.

**Wheel 91: Wheel of Efficient Use of Resources (for Rie).**
You have made yourself little because to be too bright brought criticism. No more shall My goddess be shackled. All light and all frequencies that are refined, all purified resources are yours to draw upon. As you cooperate fully with life, as you breathe in potential – we have Margaret's and Elisabeth's tied in here too- as you live this newness of being, day by day, your greatness will shine and

become glorious. Some will see light shine through your skin and they will look at you in surprise. Mother says do not do your usual and wonder - what is the matter with me, all these people looking at me a little funny? It is because they will see you as white because of the white light coming through you and you will be so glorious, goddess, that you will clear a generation of corruption but no longer as an archetype has to do it. It will happen effortlessly through the song of your heart.

## Wheel 92: Wheel of Humble Assimilation of New Potential (for Anna).

This one I really want to understand as well. I wondered, what does that mean – humble assimilation of new potential? Now Mother is going to tell us.

She says that humility is your strong suit but not as the world sees it. Not that 'I am less than another', which is simply the worship of another's arrogance, but in approaching life with the freshness of a child. I do believe that is what your husband loves about you because I have seen it in you. It is the little girl that stands in the wonderment through life. That is true humility; the acknowledging that we know nothing and that every day is new and fresh.

Mother says there are frequently light workers teaching much obsolete information because they receive a little bit of the dance of life of the potential, grabbed hold of it and then turned it into their only truth or their largest truth or a truth that is irrefutable in their minds. Mother says that in order for us to receive new fresh energy, fresh resources that youthen us to be regenerated all of the time, we need to receive not one bit of potential but the flow of it as it pours through our life and last moment's potential is already broadcast throughout the cosmos because of who you are.

You are at the epicenter and it is crystal clear to me that the group of beings that are here present, are going to be the epicenter no matter what class I teach. I have never said that before. Because I have known that every time I teach a class they are the epicenter but there are only 144 that form the epicenter. It is around that 144 that the 1440 and then the 144,000 and so on came. At the epicenter you are going to receive, not a trickle of potential, but a flood. It is in your childlike wonder that it is going to come to its heightened fruition, meaning that it is in our humility that we can use that potential the best. So that is the gift Mother gives you, this flow of new life through you.

## Wheel 103: Wheel of Boundless Growth Through Grace (for Barbara).

There couldn't have been a more valiant soldier against illusion than my sister over here. She and Anne were like hound dogs on the trail of illusion. If they got so much as the tiniest whiff of it, there they were. Illusion was not allowed in the environment. But she did it the only way we have: by turning illusion into insight, the unknown into the known which is the way of the master. This beautiful Nagual has lived impeccably in that way but it has been very tiring for her and now she gets to play and grow at the same time.

There is no limit to how far she can grow through grace. Good thing you mentioned the play. It is time for the little girl within to throw off the shackles of responsibility. It is time for others to stand on their own two feet and it is time for you to play. Growth will come through your laughter. Great vision will come through the sparkle of your eye when life is joyous to you, and where you step field flowers will grow. In other words, what Mother is saying to us is that when we fulfill, when we are all the things we want to be, life flourishes. Life flourishes, we flourish; we flourish, life flourishes. So it is time for life to flourish as she brings joy to herself.

Almine's comment: Will I tell them about Christmas? First she said "I don't dare come. My kids will throw a fit. It is quite late in

December. It's the time everybody is doing Christmas-like things."
I said, "Oh come on, we have a wonderful big tree and I'll make a
plum pudding, the works. Right now I am going to have to make a
plum pudding. Come to the Christmas POD. It is the place where the
oracles are coming, a sort of final gathering for the year. It is going
to be magnificent. We are going to do a gift exchange, fun things.
We may go Christmas caroling. Who knows what we are going to
do. We may have cookie decorating contest too." She said, "I don't
dare", but within two days she said "To heck with it, I am doing it."
Exactly what she should have done – no longer should have or could
have. Because she is going to come back and I know she is going
to have a wonderful week, her whole family will have a wonderful
week. If we are just true to ourselves, everybody else will stay at
home and have a meeting.

## Wheel 104: Wheel of Individual Relationship within the Infinite (for Natalia).

Mother says this is the fulfillment of the prophecy. OK, now which
prophecy is She talking about? When I blessed you, I said you will
help me bring the magic and you wrote me a little note to say you
were not bringing in the magic. I said you would help me do something. Mother says now is the time, it is in tomorrow's information
that is your power.

You are to thrive and you are going to bring such wonderful magic through these self wheels, Natalia, and this works for you because
it isn't outer things that need to be done, it is those of the inner,
through the lens into the within and so you are going to be extraor-
dinarily good at this.

Mother wants me to speak about your wheel. It is through the
wheel of self - the 144 wheels of the self that she will see My face
day by day and she will walk with Me and speak with Me and I will
hold her hand. Sister, that is why you have earned this! What an

exquisite gift and Mother has given it because you have exactly the right attitude and this is the attitude of greatness.

## Wheel 106: Wheel of Joyful Journey of Discovery (for Hong-An).

Oh, my gosh, Mother says it is going to be such an adventure and, make no mistake, you will be taken care of. Great developments are coming that will bring you much joy that you are manifesting powerfully in your own life. They are your heart's desires that will come to fulfillment. Many species will speak with you and you will see them. It will be a joyous adventure.

My sister's parents flew all the way in from Vietnam to see what the matter was with their daughter. She got her masters and she just brilliantly speaks fluently in multiple languages. She could go all over the world and get a highly paid job and she chose to come to Oregon to work with me for what I can afford to pay her right now. She is throwing everything to the wind because this is where her journey lies. My brothers and sisters, this courage is everywhere. This is the adventure that is coming and she is up for it

## Wheel 108: Wheel of New Creations (for Ben).

You will bring new possibilities to your life day by day through the creation of your heart if you choose to. Mother is giving you an opportunity. It is time for you to visit My holy city every day. Mother says Denis has this extraordinary oracle ability. She is a wonderful oracle and she is already going back and forth. It is time for you to go back and forth to Mother's city. There is – Mother wants me to get a word other than work – She says there is a joyous service there for you to design housing and cities for the earth's people. She gives you this wheel but the very least you will create is a beautiful life for you and your beloved.

**Wheel 109: Wheel of All Compassing Presence (for Eileen).**

This gift has two sides to it. This is a gift you can use any time you wish in the following way: the gift of all encompassing presence is the gift that allows you to be anywhere on the world that you wish. If you lie in your bed at night and you want to run with the polar bears under the Northern Lights it will be as though you are there. If you want to walk in the autumn forests of Vermont and see the colors of the landscape that are aflame, you will see it as though you are there. Mother says that if you want to imagine you are on a beach in Hawaii it is the same thing. You can be everywhere you want with real clarity. It is a gift that is in this wheel but the presence also implies the Infinite's presence and that Mother and Father are there any moment you wish to contact them. It is a type of a contact like Natalia but it is different. Natalia's is like a one-on-one contact. Yours is like a feeling of the Infinite around you. So these are the two parts that this wheel brings as a gift.

**Wheel 111: Wheel of Releasing Resistance (for Janet).**

You have been talking a lot over the years about releasing resistance. Mother is saying the releasing of resistance is for others. She says you are making a mistake. The releasing is not for you, it's for others. Wait a minute doesn't that make her an archetype? Mother says, no, it is for others in your environment. This releases flow in your environment. Mother says you do not need to have this for yourself. She says it was not Moses' power that parted the Red Sea, it was Annunaki. But it would be like the Red Sea parting in front of you. The reason this wheel is yours is because you wanted it. Mother says that life for you has had a lot of opposition over the last months and no more. So this is the wheel to part the Red Sea for you.

**Wheel 114: Wheel of One Heart Mind (for Helmut).**

It is the basis upon which the power of the first born functions. This night the pineal gland will be restructured in all beings. Mother had already done away with brain parts as being real. That was a linear relay of information. The way it was, the pineal no longer functioned. Mother says that is one of the things that is resurrected tonight and I had asked last night if it should be resurrected because I knew it was our inner sun and Mother said, "No, it is for tonight because it ushers in the power of the first born." The resurrection of the pineal gland is step one. The opening of a door in the heart is step two. She says the flow will then connect in the sternum. In the sternum a third door must open. When that third door opens the heart mind for the first time tomorrow, it will be lived by you and from you to the rest of my students and out from there to the rest of the world.

The power of the heart mind is the power of the mandala that each of you has. This mandala contains the other mandalas. You contained all the other 144 mandalas in this one because this is the place where those wheels function. They are here for all of us. My brothers and sisters, this brings up something. If you want to make your mark, and then make it into a power object, where would be the best place to wear it – on the sternum? It is a new form of cognition that allows focused intent. Remember we spoke about the focus of the ego vision. This is the lens that will open and close like the aperture of the eye to see far, to see less, to let more light in, to let less light in. It is the place of choosing vision and this is the place of the one heart mind. Extraordinary!

**Wheel 126: Wheel of Complete Trust in Divine Order (for Tadeja).** When that is in place potential flows, resources flow, and information flows because there is complete surrender. In the land in which Mother says She placed, you there has been much fearful expectation of the future. Mother says that you will be like a clear blue light upon the land as you return home. Mother says that there is a mandala that comes in terms of a saying, an aphorism that sums up the energy of this and it is something I used to say; "I am fully surrendered to life." When you know that you are all things, there is total surrender to life because everything is within and everything is changed within. It is then that you become a light torch unto all the cosmos. Mother says You are already a light torch unto all the cosmos but it will assist you in remembering Her at all times.

## Wheel 127: Wheel of Flowering (for Jerneja).

Mother says it is time. She says you will have the full measure of the blessings that you have forgone for eons of time. It is time to come home. It is time for peace to be born and joyous surrender to life (which ties in with Tadeja's). It is time for your magnificence to shine forth. My brothers and sisters I have on multiple occasions seen, just as I say these words, how we have looked to partners that are so much lower. Like a sun to a glow worm. Sometimes you don't recognize that you are in opposite matter but they do. So they push you away and you get rejected by a glow worm. Many will come to your wisdom. They should. You will teach purity.

## Wheel 134: Wheel of Restoration to Magical Life (For Helge).

He chooses his own wheel, Mother is saying. He chooses the correct wheel because he has taken every word that has been given to him deeply, reverently and seriously. For this a great blessing is given that the magic will work profoundly for him and it will work through the assistance of these wheels because it enhances the magical codes that are joined within the spine. Mother says that magical codes will not remain in the spine. They will become a field superimposed over the body but that only happens tonight. She says that the magical codes are emphasized by this wheel. Helge, it brings tears to my eyes when Mother says this because it has hurt my feelings when I have brought through in the *Arubafirina* book, the pure information

178

of these beautiful fairies. 'Arubafirina' means 'Gift of Love'. They gift us what has been most precious to them. People think – oh this is not a serious book and then they throw it down. Mother says that every word that you have heard in the class you have taken into your heart and it is for this that this gift is yours. Thank you very, very much. It means a great deal to me to work with somebody like that.

## Wheel 138: Wheel of Restoration of Magical Kingdoms (for Ines).

This is a great week for this gift to be given. She will see them but first she will hear them like Hong-An hearing the fairies. You will hear their little languages and you will draw their glyphs and it is not just the fairies, it is multiple beings. I have a stack of papers in my briefcase from the Mer People with profound information on their magic. My sister, you are going to receive the sounds and the symbols of these hidden kingdoms. I don't know which is going to come first or if they all come at once. Eventually you will see them and then you will paint them and you will restore their memories.

Let me tell you what happened here in Ireland. Eva drew these beautiful strange looking creatures. I have never seen anything like that- cute little faces that look like a flower with a little pouty mouth. I thought - Man, she doesn't draw well with this. I thought that maybe it was a drawing mistake or something that was over simplified because I couldn't imagine something looking like that. Did Mother teach me a lesson! Our sister Vanessa, who is one of the oracles of this group, was told by Leo the serpent to go to a special beach here in Ireland and that there was something she was to fetch for me there. She picked up a stone and she came sheepishly to me and said - Almine I don't know why this is going to be special to you, here is the stone and she was kind of apologetic about it. I looked at the stone and my brothers and sisters the drawing Eva made was precisely that of the fossil in the stone; even the same size. It is my pride and joy. For those of you who have been in my house recently you will have seen the paper that Eva drew and this stone lie on top of each other in a place of pride in my house. For me to actually see the physical evidence in the stone of this kingdom that she saw and drew accurately is just beyond imaginings. How beautifully exotic these kingdoms look.

You are going to bring these kingdoms to the attention of man. In addition to this, when you paint with their energy, even before you see them their frequency will start to come into our world through your paintings. You are going to, in multiple ways; work with their restoration and empowerment. This is important. Every one of the gifts Mother has given is for us, so what is in it for her? Mother says every kingdom that came is a fragment of the mirror that was dropped and the whole mirror is you. As they flourish so the different areas in your life will also.

## Wheel 142: Wheel of Limitless Creativity (for Constance).

How wonderful! This will bring joy into her home and her life with her son. All that she does will be touched if she allows this wheel to bring its creativity to her life. Rivers will flow; all stagnation will be gone in her environment as this wheel brings new creativity to life. Mother says that you have been very strong in cerebral seer-ship. This is like the flower that brings balance by raising the feminine creative side into its prominence as well. Mother says, there is no limit, because I am asking whether it is in all areas. She says there is no limit. It brings creativity to something like problem solving. Mother says there really isn't a problem you know! There never has been.

# Student Interpretation of Wheels

**Wheel 1: Wheel of Adoration of the Infinite Mother and Father. (From Ines)**
This is when you try to be who you are and do your best to realize your divinity, to know where you come from and where you are meant to be.

**Wheel 2: Wheel of Highly Refined Frequency and Light. (From Rie)**
I go to the middle of the wheel. There is a tunnel from here with light that makes the fibers in the body change the light. The wheel rotates and becomes part of awareness.

**Wheel 3: Wheel of Ultimate Refinement of Life. (From Anne)**
Eyes with ears from behind the curtains in the theatre of life see the purity of shape for ideas, all as one completely balanced.

**Wheel 4: Wheel of Passionate Exploration. (From Niels)**
Male and female accepting what lives inside of me. Both masculine and feminine, it's good and bad and the ugly and seeing what I can be even more and thus laughing all the way through it…and keep in mind that which you are not.

**Wheel 5: Wheel of Self Exploration. (From Sheila)**
The centre of this wheel looks like an eye and the different shapes and sizes suggest the many aspects of ourselves, the ability to look inward and see these different aspects, realizing we are many things. We are not static but ever changing and growing.

## Wheel 6: Wheel of Gratification in Beingness. (From Janet)

Gift in being and growing, the joyous interconnection, hallelujah, uplifted heart song fully present and presence.

## Wheel 7: Wheel of Self Courage. (From Joe)

I saw the squares turning around each other and my mind and focus was drawn to the centre. I saw that in the centre was a Maltese Cross. I remembered that the cross and the people of Malta were quite unique. As a nation during the last world war they were awarded the Victoria Cross for their courage, as they stood up to the enemy. They were never conquered and they maintained their own courage and their belief and understanding of who they were. When I looked at the Maltese cross it was surrounded by a square which appeared to enclose it. But then I noticed that the energy coming from each part of the Maltese Cross expanded and expanded the sides of the squares outward to allow them reach way beyond what they could have been before. With ourselves we remain closed in who we think we are. Yet we must go beyond the walls that keep us enclosed. When we have the courage to do that, we take on our real identity and this allows us to become all we can be without limitation.

## Wheel 9: Wheel of Self Knowledge. (From Elisabeth, Germany)

Know this self but know that you don't know, feel who you are within your heart. Know that I am on your side. Why are you questioning yourself? Question yourself on your pathway with patience and self love. Although never forget who you are, questioning yourself is stimulating growth and I am growing with you.

## Wheel 10: Wheel of Self Gratitude. (From Natalia)

There is always reason to be grateful; expressing gratitude to self by using self wheel to make celebration I put myself in the middle of the wheel circle pentagon five point stars and diamonds and pull the light through all these portals. These are the highest way to experience feelings of gratitude giving possibility to express gratitude to others.

### Wheel 12: Wheel of Self Celebration. (From Tadeja)

Do not forget about me. Celebrate for what you have been through and for what is yet to come.

### Wheel 14: Wheel of Self Grace. (From Barbara)

Grace is the combination of all the purest qualities of the divine. It fills me, flows through me and from me. Every cell of my being is grace and that grace nurtures and sustains me, fuelling my passion to be more. Knowing I am eternally fed, grace pours forth from me enabling all to see and feel the grace within and around them, and in turn grace is reflected back to me.

### Wheel 15: Wheel of Self Sustenance. (From Maureen)

From the center deep and dark the light thrusts forward right and left, high and low. Filling the wheel with flowers and fans, filigrees of lace, strong strokes long, and reach out across the radius of the self filling the wheel with all that's needed to fulfill soul, self and sustenance.

### Wheel 16: Wheel of Integrated Oneness. (From Marian)

A feeling of infinity, each part of the pattern is complete and whole in itself but allows itself to continue and move and then move through to create a unified whole.

### Wheel 17: Wheel of Fire Within. (From Ben)

We live with passion according to our heart flame. We also nurture that flame inside us. We use the flame as a form of nourishment rather than a destructive force.

## Wheel 18: Wheel of Self Truth. (From Eileen)

In the centre is the black square containing a flower. For self-truth? I must stand in the black square of humanity while celebrating my divine flower in the centre.

## Wheel 19: Wheel of Self Trust. (From Anna)

The old way of seeing through earlier mistakes, destroy self trust. The new way is the light of Mother, self trust is flowering.

## Wheel 20: Wheel of Self Generated Resource. (From Natalia)

In this wheel I am placing myself in the middle of the wheel of eight star center and passing through mind all departments; this give you possibility to generate unlimited resource for realization of your passion.

## Wheel 21: Wheel of Entrained Frequency. (From Helmut)

Simultaneous unfolding flowering of the rose, synchronized light pulsation eliciting spontaneous creations by the flow of the Infinite Heart.

## Wheel 22: Wheel of Innocence. (From Rie)

I go to the Centre of this wheel. In the middle of my heart there is silence and everything goes out from there. I feel the vertical and horizontal direction of life goes from my heart. There is no analyzing, just being in the moment, like seeing through the eyes of a child.

## Wheel 23: Wheel of Purity. (From Marian)

Purity of intent - it acts like a laser beam that cuts through what is known to bring us to the unknown. There lies pristineness.

## Wheel 24: Wheel of Adoration in Action. (From Anna)

Adoration is communication with the Infinite. My heart is singing.

**Wheel 25: Wheel of Regeneration. (From Sheila)**
Actual regeneration of self by looking or going inward, the eye is directed inward to the middle of the wheel which for me says look inward and not out to others.

**Wheel 26: Wheel of Self Respect. (From Gaby)**
Claiming and being at home, at one with your divinity, evolving precise, harmonious boundaries, giving structure to your beauty, honoring the self uplifts all life.

**Wheel 27: Wheel of Self Directed Desire of the Heart. (From Hong-An)**
Live in the moment, without thinking of past or future and spontaneously follow your heart at the moment, effortlessly without resistance. Ask yourself - what is my heart's desire to do at this moment? Trust what your inner voice is telling you. It is always positive and gentle and then follow it. Gifts and opportunities will show up when you follow the heart's desire in the moment. Trust the inner and what the inner voice tells you

**Wheel 29: Wheel of Self Mastery in Action. (From Denis)**
We live in silence of the mind in fluidity, in assimilation, integrity, love with open heart, open mind we leave our imprint in the cosmos.

**Wheel 30: Wheel of Self Seeing Perfection. (From Rose)**
We are all made in the image of the Infinite. Therefore we are all perfect. See the perfection of all because Mother does not make mistakes.

**Wheel 31: Wheel of Compassionate Understanding. (From Joe)**
When I looked at the wheel it looked as if one side corresponded to the other but in the middle there was a gap that looked like a zip that had

broken and was bulging outward. This created the separation from one side to the other. I can hold up a page to a person and ask them what they see and they will give me and idea of what they think. But I can see the other side. Looking at the same page but from a different perspective it will seem completely different. I need to walk around to the other side to understand what it is the person is seeing and feeling and in this way I can have a better understanding and I know then where the person is coming from. In this way, there is no judgment and I can be completely compassionate in my understanding of that person.

### Wheel 33: Wheel of Self Acceptance. (From Geraldine)
To have self-acceptance we need to be aware of who we are at the moment. Our thoughts and feeling and our physical sensations we trust and accept. This wheel has a flavor in the center that pulses into the very core of existence. It feels that as we accept ourselves we grow into the essence of who we are - a sense of being free from conditioning of society, and agendas of people around us

### Wheel 35: Wheel of Self Belief. (From Elisabeth, Germany)
Believe in yourself as I believe in you. Believe that you are embedded in the love of the divine Mother and Father. Believe in yourself and feel their guidance. Believe in yourself and ask for my hand, the angel Shambalek, we walk together.

### Wheel 36: Wheel of Self Determination. (From Anna)
It is hard work to reach your goals in the new way, the discipline of being in the now, joy in the moment.

### Wheel 37: Wheel of Interconnectedness. (From Marian)
A flower, every thing, petal of this flower which to me represents each and every one of us holds a different pattern. Yet we all become one where the petals meet in the centre through holding and honor-

ing the pattern or gift. We allow ourselves to flower and connect through our uniqueness.

### Wheel 38: Wheel of Self Motivation. (From Gaby)

Spontaneous disciplined creations, focused intent, manifesting heart's desire, empowering all life with your self-love and freedom.

### Wheel 39: Wheel of Pristine Co-existence with Nature. (From Cory)

We are part of the web which is totally balanced, strong, spacious, interrelated and interdependent.

### Wheel 40: Wheel of Self Accomplishment. (From Elizabeth, Ireland)

This mandala is the thousand lotus flower and I am the diamond in the center of the flower like the jewel in the crown, drawing the energy from the divine in the center and flowing in all directions, like life. The shapes change from moment to moment.

### Wheel 42: Wheel of Self Light in Beingness. (From Natalia)

I am light in my beingness and the endless source of creation and magic. Whenever I wish I can go and stay in beingness and increase the source. In the wheel, there are twelve portions of my light to manifest. It divided and every time I use the wheel, I put myself in the entry of the ray tunnel and fill pulsation and five circles around me until I feel one with the ray and we pull deeper looking how the light with different colors going through me. In the same way I am going through another level like tunnels enjoying experience. All needs to look after other, sources of light are released.

### Wheel 43: Wheel of Self Perception. (From Constance)

A lotus that is in flames and it reaches outward surrounded by circles like theatre curtain, at times it is beautiful and other times sinister.

**Wheel 44: Wheel of Unlimited Access to Knowledge. (From Helge)**
It reminds me of the womb of a woman, the hole through is a follicle. The small one is an unripe follicle. Then it becomes bigger and the oval in the middle is the ripe follicle popping up and out with the new knowledge. It is about creating new knowledge beyond the forefront to be well integrated to the Mother. It is an exploration, a discovery. It is about creating. When I last looked at it suddenly matter and light popped out around me and in the forefront and in the background. It is about being conscious in all levels and places, a strong moral connection.

**Wheel 45: Wheel of Experiential Knowledge. (From Angela)**
One is four until it hits the void to merge into one birthing form, yet sharing of segments surrounding what is the beginning of alternating movement.

**Wheel 46: Wheel of Self Dignity. (From Rose)**
Have dignity in everything we create or experience. There are no wrongs or rights. Everything flows with divine perfection.

**Wheel 47: Wheel of Fluidity in Mastery. (From Ellen)**
Living from the heart being fluid, willing to change in the moment, trusting in the perfection of life, no hesitation, going with the flow, yesterday's truth may not be today's truth.

**Wheel 48: Wheel of Self Discovery. (From Tadeja)**
Stop resisting against what you think or mark as bad. Inner voice criticism will get silent.

**Wheel 49: Wheel of Devoted Service to the Infinite Mother and Father. (From Ines)**

Devoted is to be who you are and to let Mother and Father know that. Then you become a part of Them and then a part of you into infinity.

**Wheel 50: Wheel of Appreciation of Self Perfection. (From Niels)**

Self perfection - realize it is already there in me, so take time for myself. I know it is not always easy to be here. Acknowledge the heroism of everyday life. It is ok to give yourself a little pat on the back for kicking some serious illusion back. So appreciate yourself in the biggest sense of the word for you are perfection.

**Wheel 51: Wheel of Appreciating Self in External Beauty. (From Geraldine)**

We can appreciate and indeed connect with our internal beauty, by appreciating the way in our lives; we express our internal beauty - in how we treat ourselves, others and the environment. As we allow pure love and light to pour through our hearts we connect with internal beauty that is present in a flower, in the eyes of a child, beauty of the Infinite in all of life.

**Wheel 52: Wheel of Plentiful Supply. (From Helmut)**

It is the playful invitation to completely welcome the undoubted joyful potential.

**Wheel 53: Wheel of Appreciating Beauty. (From Helena)**

Appreciating beauty - it has recognizing and seeing beauty within us and around us. It is recognizing perfection of that creation through us. It is a way to express our delight. It is a joyful way to nourish our hearts.

### Wheel 54: Wheel of Self Guidance. (From Sheila)

This wheel goes with regeneration in that we listen to our hearts to guide us to our highest. It is symbolic of a fan that turns around a central core of the heart. Without that core there is no movement.

### Wheel 55: Wheel of Self Acknowledgement. (From Rie)

There is joy, peace, relaxation and a home feeling that opens the body. There is a lot of space, everything tightness in the muscles goes away. I am perfect just as I am.

### Wheel 56: Wheel of Self Generated Focus in Life. (From Annette)

Layer behind layer energy growth sharpens. A green field full of blooming flowers feeling the sun warming my body and the opening of the heart. There is only light and silence of the mind.

### Wheel 57: Wheel of Peaceful Desires of the Heart. (From Anna)

In the old way of seeing, it is difficult to do good things in the world when we are only sitting still and peaceful. In the new way it is flowering and being in the now.

### Wheel 58: Wheel of Balance in Motion. (From Jerneja)

This wheel is symbolizing beautiful dancing.

### Wheel 60: Wheel of Self Appreciation. (From Annette)

Love, balance, life, beautifulness, the feeling of my wings growing, flying, looking down on the landscape below and there is only oneness.

### Wheel 62: Wheel of Self Reliance. (From Carmel)

This wheel represents a layer of self which needs to be uncovered to build self reliance from our inner core. The power of self reliance is to continually go deeper within to a place of complete self awareness, understanding and love, continually building our inner strength.

## Wheel 63: Wheel of Acknowledging of Self Contributions. (From Geraldine)

How often we live on auto-pilot in a place of mindless activity. We use ourselves, the mothers who cook countless dinners, the fathers who take the children to football matches, the healers, the teachers all contributing enormous gifts to the planet, the cosmos. When we acknowledge our kindness we embody kindness. As we acknowledge our trust we embody trust. So then the values of our contributions are multiplied thousand of times. The entire cosmos is empowered and expanded.

## Wheel 64: Wheel of Seeing Value in All Life. (From Gregory)

It is associated with many facets and more stars within us, this represents that, when we see the value in anything. It has many facets that a man who has a handful of sand can find more joy watching it pouring through his fingers than the man who owns the beach. Seeing the value in all life grants us innocence and non judgment of good or bad, for all life is good.

## Wheel 65: Wheel of Unified Fields. (From Carmel)

These three ringed wheels represent the unification of the male and the female aspects within the self, the unification of self within the cosmos and the unification of the cosmos within the loving embrace of the Mother.

## Wheel 66: Wheel of Exponential Growth. (From Joe)

The center is like a burst of energy that as it spreads out it forms stars, multifaceted stars and these again were surrounded by a greater multifaceted star also. Around each star point are spirals which signify infinity. So with this we have the ability to not enclose ourselves in limitation but know that we have stages of development and it is a never ending journey of growth, of awareness, of evolution.

### Wheel 67: Wheel of Self Awareness. (From Helena)

We walk through life as masters being conscious of not knowing. We gracefully walk with the flow and total surrender to the moment. As we walk our paths we listen, assimilate and act with the mind and the heart as one.

### Wheel 68: Wheel of Birthing New Paradigms. (From Jerneja)

Let all birthing be full of passion and freedom

### Wheel 69: Wheel of Self Empowerment. (From Annette)

Strength, happiness, adjustment to put the full elements in balance, walking on the beach feeling the sun, I am smelling and hearing the ocean while long strings of silver connect me to the universe and the center of earth.

### Wheel 70: Wheel of Purification through Gratitude. (From Gregory)

There is a flower growing outwards. It shows that gratitude helps us to be lighter out in the world, to be grateful for our tears which cleanse us and for our soul that chose happiness or amusement and grants us purity and mastery in gratitude for any object of any size.

### Wheel 71: Wheel of Luminous Living. (From Ellen)

Coming out of the web of illusion, going into the unknown, we let our light shine brightly in every area of our lives.

**Wheel 72: Wheel of Self Recognition of Uniqueness. (From Tadeja)**

Old stories of comparison of what existed are over. It's the place where you never find yourself. My unique me, is in my heart, open heart and open mind.

**Wheel 73: Wheel of Integrated Sub-personalities. (From Hong-An)**

We have four sub-personalities: warrior and nurturer, the elder and child. Recently warrior and nurturer merged into one and elder and child merged into one. Elder teaches child wisdom, while child provides youthfulness to elder.

Warrior is masculine counterpart to nurturer, while nurturer takes care of warrior's spirit. Since the Infinite is androgynous, it is time to integrate both of the merged sub-personalities to feel balanced. Make sure of balanced relationship between warrior and nurturer and elder and child and then integrate all within us to maintain androgyny.

**Wheel 74: Wheel of Embracing Life. (From Niels)**

The essence is rich fluidity and joy. Embracing life is not, thinking that you know, because then you embrace belief systems and then you embrace labels. See beyond that. See a tree for the first time. See its divine grace and power. Getting to the negative and positive side of life, don't be afraid of it. Enjoy and have fun unencumbered by how things should be – one big joyous adventure.

**Wheel 75: Wheel of Inclusiveness. (From Cory)**

As we expand we are being safely held. We dance out through the cosmos to touch the edge and then back to the centre.

**Wheel 77: Wheel of Enthusiastic Surrender to the Now. (From Elisabeth, Germany)**

This is knowing, feeling, understanding, embracing, loving, celebrating and flowing with enthusiastic surrender in the moment which is present, past and after. Surrender into the flow of the now.

**Wheel 79: Wheel of Self Stability through Faith. (From Anne)**

Faith is that heaven is in the heart, living and communicating from the heart will stabilize your life.

**Wheel 80: Wheel of Self Assurance through Humility. (From Janet)**

Assimilation of new potential, by moving out of creating dysfunctionality in our lives and by taking what we learned, we can create new potential in all the areas.

**Wheel 81: Wheel of Listening with the Heart. (From Helmut)**

Pure openness, allowing open receptivity arising from the softest most intimate fluid stillness, delicate ability emerges silently, dwelling in the core of love.

**Wheel 85: Wheel of Co-Operative Endeavors. (From Hong-An)**

Whatever project or activity one takes, the most important thing is to follow your heart and be open to any opportunities, help from the universe. It is based on giving and receiving; where the person and the universe are working together in the person's endeavors whether it is a vision quest, hobby, career, spending time with children, or going with the flow of oneself and the universe.

**Wheel 89: Wheel of Interpretative Dance. (From Barbara)**

My dance is my fluid interpretation of all that I am and all that I am becoming. As I move to the beat and swell of my heart. As my heart sings its own song I hear and understand it and so the rest of my being moves to the music and as it does it co-operates with and enhances all life.

## Wheel 97: Wheel of Self Wisdom. (From Constance)

I can see the wheel clearly with eyes wide open but when I try to focus it becomes sinister. Therefore it is saying we must keep our eyes open at all times.

## Wheel 98: Wheel of Self Assessment. (From Helge)

The ability to see where you are, to know what is going on as you are doing from your heart and you are looking from a higher perspective to know what to do next.

## Wheel 99: Wheel of Simplicity of Choices. (From Constance)

The absolute simplicity of the picture, what I love, is its simplicity when I looked at it. I see lines like shadows, like other lifetimes; there was one formation that was clearly there. This is the choice that we have made with this lifetime. It is irrefutable and undeniable we have made our choices already and we reject complexity that we keep creating, we find peace in the choices made.

## Wheel 100: Wheel of Freedom from Nostalgia of the Past. (From Barbara)

Yes, we had wonderful past memories and these have been made wonderful by rose tinted glasses. To hold onto them however limits our capacity to fully engage in the beauty in the here and now as the old becomes the lens through which we view this moment. I am now free to fully experience and enjoy this moment as it unfolds untainted by what has been. I live fully in the here and now recognizing it as my springboard to greater passion, joy and love.

**Wheel 102: Wheel of Creating New Memories. (From Denis)**
What we create now ripples backward into the past; new present – new past.

**Wheel 104: Wheel of Individual Relationship with the Infinite. (From Angela)**
Inside the womb of creation, the chambers held where the one begins to spiral from the centre point. As it moves it discovers its own creation of flow spiraling up to the umbilical cord until it finds where it is held. It is Mother.

**Wheel 110: Wheel of Releasing Duty. (From Ben)**
Duty is a form of programming and as such it must be let go. We will live life with our heart thereby transmuting duty to desire.

**Wheel 111: Wheel of Releasing Resistance. (From Eileen)**
The design flows outwards and makes me feel that I am standing in the middle of a fountain of beautiful liquid which constantly washes away my resistance.

**Wheel 113: Wheel of Self Manifested Intent. (From Anne)**
Everything ripples out from a small spark into the heart, growing more powerful and beautiful as it flows effortlessly outward to create our desires.

**Wheel 114: Wheel of One Heart Mind. (From Anne)**
The wisdom of the eye is overseeing the heart of man and creating the form of the Infinite within the cosmos.

**Wheel 115: Wheel of Pristine Creations. (From Ines)**
This is when the music of the spheres, that beautiful and unspeak-

able energy, the music of Mother and Father's heart, is going to my heart and then everything is possible

**Wheel 116: Wheel of Imaginative Expression. (From Maureen)**
Commas and dots, circles and exclamations, all ordinary ways of communication are brought together by the imagination to imitate the wonders of great Mother's creation. In the circle of this wheel, I can play recreating Mother's order with my small imagination.

**Wheel 120: Wheel of Communion with the Infinite. (From Elizabeth, Ireland)**
To me the name communion represents common man and the union that everyone is entitled to the Infinite energy. The mandala itself looks like a complicated web of energy. A little like life, but upon further investigation, while it has many doorways, many triangles and many lines as it pulsates in color and shape, the spider web becomes very obvious. From the central point the divine energy appears. The thousands of strands around the central point represent all of our communication with the Divine and this spreads out through to the universe.

**Wheel 121: Wheel of Complete Release. (From Gregory)**
This releases us of old patterns and frees us of agendas that we live in every day of our lives, to free us to be spontaneous, to free us from suppression and to allow us to be as before.

**Wheel 123: Wheel of Dissolving Obsolete Patterns. (From Janet)**
By learning lessons well we can then let go of old patterns that created dysfunction in our lives. By doing so we are helping others.

**Wheel 124: Wheel of Unlimited Learning. (From Janet)**
It is a web, endless. We know everything yet we know nothing.

**Wheel 125: Wheel of Dissolving Dysfunctionality. (From Janet)**
Even when there is dysfunction in all areas of our life we can still learn valuable lessons, see the beauty. Once we can see this, then we can dissolve the dysfunctionality we no longer need.

**Wheel 126: Wheel of Complete Trust in Divine Order. (From Jerneja)**
When I lose trust, I feel tension, control, fear and worry. When I recall trust all of these feelings disappear and I can just relax and enjoy life as a journey.

**Wheel 130: Wheel of Full Emotional Expression. (From Rose)**
All emotional expressions are positive and perfectly balanced. None should be denied. Embrace all emotions with the essence of excitement and adventure.

**Wheel 131: Wheel of Eternal Life. (From Ellen)**
Living in the now, in the moment, no beginning or end, no looking back or forward, living in the silence of the mind, living from the heart.

**Wheel 133: Wheel of Physical Manifestation. (From Helena)**
We are the foundation of the physical manifestation. This is acknowledging power within us. It is an enormous privilege and opportunity to change our environment by changing within us. This is a glorious gift of the creation's ability, limitless to manifest our intent and heart as desired.

**Wheel 134: Wheel of Restoration to Magical Life. (From Angela)**
Love in the centre with balance straight down the stem. As it goes down it gives birth to spirals that expand beyond time, for below the circles gives rise to looking for kingdoms that are originated from love.

**Wheel 136: Wheel of Becoming Divine Architects. (From Ben)**
We create the future by our thoughts. We are also way-showers of those plans to assist others in their spiritual lives.

**Wheel 137: Wheel of Instant Access to Infinite Knowledge. (From Eileen)**
There are two large concentric circles like two big eyes. I am drawn to the black space between them which make them seem like emptiness. What is fullness?

**Wheel 138: Wheel of Restoration of Magical Kingdoms. (From Maureen)**
A carpet of flowers great and small, each a symbol of the kingdom of magic coming forth from the lost places of the earth and beyond calling me to make a place, a space, a circle on land to welcome the magical kingdoms on my land in Wicklow.

**Wheel 139: Wheel of Dissolving Stagnant Boundaries. (From Denis)**
We leave the old way breaking all unconstructive former agreements; we go with the flow of life.

**Wheel 140: Wheel of Dissolving Programming. (From Carmel)**
This wheel represents a complex pattern of fine threads woven together like a spider's web. Awareness is courage to pull the thread, dissolving forever the programming of the past that holds us back from being what we truly are.

**Wheel 143: Wheel of Unobstructed Vision. (From Cory)**
It is seeing through every layer and in the distance having a total range of focus to be able to see the microcosm, macrocosm, infinity.

**Wheel 144: Wheel of Everlasting Guidance by the Infinite. (From Elizabeth, Ireland)**

A profound mandala with the old seeing eye of god in the centre on the perimeter, eight eyes above, below, to the sides the all seeing eyes. From the all seeing eyes are the kundalini spiraling energies going right out the perimeter which is guarded by male and female, Mother and Father. The mandala is represented by eight layers going upwards and to me eight is the number of infinity.

# The One Wheel That Contains All

# Closing

What greater gift can we give another, than the gift of enlightenment? Through ages of being in stages of deep forgetfulness, called the Great Fall, the cosmos has emerged into a state of Ascension. Growth used to come through opposition and insights lay hidden in the adversities of our lives.

This is no longer so. Growth now comes through grace and support[9]; one of the many reasons so many sacred tools are being given to man. Effortless knowing has replaced delving for insights through the painful experiences of our lives. The greater the service we render, the more profound the enlightenment to us.

Kaanish Belvaspata is the vehicle to make a profound impact not only on others but also on the practitioners who use it. Each time it is used, it brings us closer to personal mastery; that state of being in which we see from all perspectives at once and have the option to function from the silence of the mind.

May we receive it with gratitude, acknowledging with honor and respect its holy origin as a gift from the Infinite Being.

In love, praise and gratitude,
Almine

---

9 See *The Thought that Fractured the Infinite*

## Other books by Almine

### The Ring of Truth *Third Edition*
**Sacred Secrets of the Goddess**

As man slumbers in awareness, the nature of his reality has altered forever. As one of the most profound mystics of all time, Almine explains this dramatic shift in cosmic laws that is changing life on earth irrevocably. A powerful healing modality is presented to compensate for the changes in laws of energy, healers have traditionally relied upon. The new principles of beneficial white magic and the massive changes in spiritual warriorship are meticulously explained.

Published: 2009, 256 pages, soft cover, 6 x 9, ISBN: 978-1-934070-28-4

### The Thought that Fractured the Infinite
**The Genesis of Individuated Life**

This profound work offers insights where few authors dare to tread: the genesis of individuated life.
Offering what could possibly be the deepest insights ever revealed about man's relationship to light, it details our ascent into spiritual awakening.
It gives the thought-provoking wisdom of the cosmic root races and a practical guide to using the alchemical potencies of light. Almine's global following of serious students of the mysteries will love this one!

Published: 2009, 316 pages, soft cover, 6 x 9, ISBN: 978-1-934070-17-8

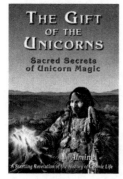

### The Gift of the Unicorns *Second Edition*
**Sacred Secrets of Unicorn Magic**

These life-changing insights into the deep mystical secrets of the earth's past puts the cosmic role of humanity into perspective. It gives meaning to the suffering of the ages and solutions of hope and predicts the restoration of white magic. An enlightening explanation of the causes of the Great Fall and our ascent out of ages of forgetfulness into a remembrance of our divine new purpose and oneness, is masterfully given. Truly an inspiring book!

Published: 2009, 284 pages, soft cover, 6 x 9, ISBN: 978-1-934070-29-1

## Other books by Almine

## Opening the Doors of Heaven *Second Edition*
### Revelations of the Mysteries of Isis
Through a time-travel tunnel, linking Ireland and Egypt, Isis sent a small group of masters to prepare for the day when her mysteries would once again be released to the world to restore balance and enhance life.

They established the Order of the White Rose to guard the sacred objects and the secrets of Isis. In an unprecedented event heralding the advent of a time of light, these mysteries are released for the first time.

Published: 2009, 312 pages, soft cover, 6 x 9 ISBN: 978-1-934070-31-4

## Windows Into Eternity *Second Edition*
### Revelations of the Mother Goddess
This book provides unparalled insight into ancient mysteries. Almine, an internationally recognized mystic and teacher, reveals the hidden laws of existence. Transcending reason, delivering visionary expansion, this metaphysical masterpiece explores the origins of life as recorded in the Holy Libraries.
The release of information from these ancient libraries is a priceless gift to humankind. The illusions found in the building blocks of existence are exposed, as are the purposes of Creation.

Published: 2009, 320 pages, soft cover, 6 x 9, ISBN: 978-1-934070-32-1

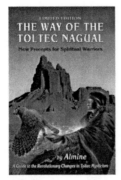

## The Way of the Toltec Nagual
### New Precepts for the Spiritual Warrior
Not only is this wisdom packed book a guide for serious students of the Toltec way, but also a font of knowledge for all truth-seekers. Mapping out the revolutionary changes in Toltec mysticism, it presents the precepts of mastery sought out by all who travel the road of illumination and spiritual warriorship. Almine reveals publicly for the first time, the ancient power symbols used by Toltec Naguals to assist in obtaining freedom from illusion. Bonus section: Learn about the hidden planets used by Toltecs and the Astrology of Isis.

Published: 2009, 240 pages, soft cover, 6 x 9, ISBN: 978-1-934070-56-7

# Other books by Almine

## A Life of Miracles
### *Expanded Third Edition* **Includes Bonus Belvaspata Section—Mystical Keys to Ascension**
Almine's developing spiritual awareness and abilities from her childhood in South Africa until she emerged as a powerful mystic, to devote her gifts in support of all humanity is traced. Deeply inspiring and unique in its comparison of man's relationship as the microcosm of the macrocosm. *Also available in Spanish.*

Published: 2009, 304 pages, soft cover, 6 x 9, ISBN: 978-1-934070-25-3

## Journey to the Heart of God *Second Edition*
### Mystical Keys to Immortal Mastery
Ground-breaking cosmology revealed for the first time, sheds new light on previous bodies of information such as the Torah, the I Ching and the Mayan Zolkien. The explanation of man's relationship as the microcosm as set out in the previous book *A Life of Miracles*, is expanded in a way never before addressed by New Age authors, giving new meaning and purpose to human life. Endorsed by an Astro-physicist from Cambridge University and a former NASA scientist, this book is foundational for readers at all levels of spiritual growth.

Published: 2009, 296 pages, soft cover, 6 x 9, ISBN: 978-1-934070-26-0

## Secrets Of The Hidden Realms *Second Edition*
### Mystical Keys to the Unseen Worlds
This remarkable book delves into mysteries few mystics have ever revealed. It gives in detail: *The practical application of the goddess mysteries • Secrets of the angelic realms • The maps, alphabets, numerical systems of Lemuria, Atlantis, and the Inner Earth • The Atlantean calender, accurate within 5 minutes • The alphabet of the Akashic libraries. Secrets of the Hidden Realms* is a truly amazing bridge across the chasm that has separated humanity for eons from unseen realms.

Published: 2009, 412 pages, soft cover, 6 x 9, ISBN: 978-1-934070-27-7

## CDs by Almine

*Each powerful presentation has a unique musical background unaltered as channeled from Source. Truly a work of art.*

### The Power of Silence
Few teaching methods empty the mind, but rather fill it with more information. As one who has achieved this state of silence, Almine meticulously maps out the path that leads to this state of expanded awareness.

### The Power of Self-Reliance
Cultivating self-reliance is explained as resulting from balancing the sub-personalities—key components to emotional autonomy.

### Mystical Keys to Ascended Mastery
The way to overcome and transcend mortal boundaries is clearly mapped out for the sincere truth seeker.

### The Power of Forgiveness
Digressing from traditional views that forgives a perceived injury, this explains the innocence of all experience. Instead of showing how to forgive a wrong, it acknowledges wholeness.

## Visit Almine's websites:

www.astrology-of-isis.com

www.arubafirina.com

www.ascensionangels.com

www.alminehealing.com

www.ascendedmastery.com

www.lifeofmiracles.com

www.mysticalkingdoms.com

www.earthwisdomchronicles.com

www.divinearchitect.com

www.incorruptiblewhitemagic.com

www.wheelsofthegoddess.com

www.ancientshamanism.com

www.wayofthetoltecnagual.com

www.schoolofarcana.org

www.belvaspata.org

Diary: www.alminediary.com

www.spiritual-healing-for-animals.com

Visit Almine's website **www.spiritualjourneys.com** for workshop locations and dates, take an online workshop, listen to an internet radio show, or watch a video. Order one of Almine's many books, CD's, or an instant download.

Phone Number: 1-877-552-5646

LaVergne, TN USA
08 October 2010

200079LV00004B/2/P

9 781934 070444